"Transformation–the distinct shift into a markedly better mindset or behavior by a work team at any level–is that almost magical breakthrough all managers and change facilitators aspire for but seldom consciously achieve.

In this practical but pathfinding book, Douglas O'Loughlin shares 12 key strategies from his deep and extensive experience into the alchemy of achieving that critical shift for better performance. This is a great handbook for all managers written by an outstanding change facilitator and management educator."

– **Yeoh Lam Keong**, Director of Economics and Strategy
Government Investment Corporation (GIC)

"Doug is a great facilitator–we have always learned a lot from him and he never fails to energize us with activities, processes, stories, etc. That is the reason why we keep inviting him back. The 12 strategies in this book provide a valuable roadmap for people who have the desire to expand their effectiveness as facilitators."

– **Chong Siak Ching**, President and CEO
Ascendas

"I admire and respect Doug because of his integrity and deep love of people. Having watched him during many presentations, his understanding of human affairs and organizational dynamics are topped only by his magical pedagogy and insights which he has built into the seemingly innocuous chapter titles of this book. His writing, as his teaching, is an expression of 'profound simplicity', created by his teaching and facilitating, as well as being a walking example of his philosophy and convictions. This book will be your constant travelling companion for the work you do."

– **Horst Abraham,** Adjunct Faculty
University of Michigan–Executive Education

"In our hands is a valuable resource containing the experiences, insights and wisdom of an extraordinary facilitator. Trainers, facilitators, and even participants will benefit from the 12 strategies that Douglas has generously put together for all of us!"

– **Michael Boey,** First Vice-President
Learning and Organization Development, United Overseas Bank Group

"Doug has assisted many of our major clients with his insights and practical advices on creating transformation. I have seen how he almost instantaneously creates a 'connection' and chemistry with his audience, and how he manages group engagement to enhance buy-in. I highly recommend this book, written by an extraordinary and knowledgeable practitioner, to anyone desiring to learn how to facilitate team transformation!"

– **Asad Zaidi**, Chief Executive Officer
MDi Pakistan

"Doug has supported our business as a facilitator and coach for several years. Facilitation is both a science and an art, and Doug is the ultimate artist who has the ability to engage everyone in the room. After adopting his strategies, we've managed to steer our team through a challenging period and emerged as a stronger unit with a passion for our people, performance and profits!"

– **Andrew Linfoot**, Director
& **Jolene Loh,** Head of Business Development
Pacific Life Re Asia

"This book is packed with simple and yet profound ideas for being a catalyst for transformation. I have had the great pleasure to work with Douglas on several projects in the last ten years, each one a unique and customized experience. I have also witnessed many transformational experiences where individuals and organizations have been positively impacted after attending Douglas' workshops."

– **John Mauro**
Surveys@Work

"I am glad that Douglas has finally sat down and distilled his years of masterful facilitation experience into this book. He was instrumental in bringing me into the facilitation world, as I was greatly impacted by his humility and the miracles I saw in the sessions he facilitated. After more than twenty years, he remains a close and treasured friend."

– **Prabu Naidu**
Learning Matters and Facilitators Network of Singapore (FNS)

"Doug is a great Organization Development (OD) coach and facilitator whom I've worked with for more than 10 years. His passion, belief and ability to connect with all levels of employees, and ability to influence and inspire them, is what makes the programs he designed for us and our partnership a success. He takes no shortcut but invests lots and lots of time and energy with the participants before and after the sessions. This book offers excellent guidelines on how this success can be replicated."

– **Cindy Wee,** Asia Regional HR Leader
Marsh

"I have partnered with Douglas in various organizational change programs in different industries. His passion for transformation at both the personal and organizational level has created breakthroughs with diverse groups. He has the masterful facilitation skills and abilities to match this passion. You will uncover useful tips in this book for leading individuals and companies through transformational change."

– **TP Tay,** Vice-President of Human Resources
Japfa Comfeed International

"With this book Douglas O'Loughlin challenges and inspires facilitators and trainers to expect more from themselves and from their participants. The 12 strategies present great insights on how to co-create shifts in work and life with participants. The book is filled with lots of practical insights, personal experiences, exercises and a useful list of references for further reading. We highly recommend this book to anyone–regardless of your experience level–who works as a facilitator, trainer, coach or teacher. This is a book about transformation, this is a book about life, and this is a book that is transformational by itself."

– **Aart and Loes Pijl**
Change Company

First published October 2009
Reprinted May 2010

FACILITATING TRANSFORMATION

12 STRATEGIES FOR CREATING EXTRAORDINARY BREAKTHROUGHS WITH GROUPS

Author : Douglas O'Loughlin
Publisher : Phoon Kok Hwa
Cover design : Lim Siew Yuen
Layout : Janny Jin
Published by : Candid Creation Publishing
524, Kampong Bahru Road, #03-00
Singapore 099455
Website : www.SingaporeBookPublisher.com
Email : enquiry@SingaporeBookPublisher.com
ISBN : 978-981-08-3040-3

National Library Board Singapore Cataloguing in Publication Data

O'Loughlin, Douglas.
Facilitating transformation : 12 strategies for creating extraordinary breakthroughs with groups / Douglas O'Loughlin.–Singapore : Candid Creation Pub., 2009.
p. cm.
ISBN-13 : 978-981-08-3040-3 (pbk.)

1. Group facilitation. 2. Transformative learning. I. Title.

HM751
302.34 -- dc22 OCN440640592

Printed on Cyclus Offset 100% recycled paper
Printed and bound in Singapore

FACILITATING TRANSFORMATION

12 STRATEGIES FOR CREATING EXTRAORDINARY BREAKTHROUGHS WITH GROUPS

Douglas O'Loughlin

Candid Creation Publishing

TABLE OF CONTENTS

FOREWORD

To all colleagues who aspire to facilitate transformation, here is the first stanza of a poem by Rudyard Kipling, entitled "IF", written in 1896. See if you can identify with these words:

> If you can keep your head when all about you
> Are losing theirs and blaming it on you;
> If you can trust yourself when all men doubt you,
> But make allowance for their doubting too;
> If you can wait and not be tired of waiting,
> Or being lied about, don't deal in lies,
> Or being hated, don't give way to hating,
> And yet don't look too good, nor talk too wise;

The other stanzas of the poem offer similar challenges for consideration. Kipling concludes with,

> Yours is the Earth and everything in it,
> And–which is more–you'll be a man, my son!

Many of us know what it is like to stand in front of a group encountering disorder, confusion, apathy or frustration. Under such situations, it is difficult to imagine that new discoveries and creative solutions can be a product of such chaos. If, as Doug (and Kipling) suggests, we can stay present and intentional, mindful of our plan and capable of spontaneity, there is a high probability that we can guide people to a new way of seeing themselves, their system and their task. We can then change the last line to read... "And–which is more–you'll be a Facilitator, my friend!"

As facilitators, we learn to live with perceived contradictions. While facilitation is an expression of our most creative selves, it is a science grounded in decades of research. While we are often called upon to be at the center of the action, we remain astute observers and hold the bigger picture. While we invest ourselves emotionally in our clients, we remain objective and respectful of the work they have to do for themselves. While we plan carefully, we learn to trust our intuition as to when to deviate from our plan.

Many of us chose this work because we want to enable people to make discoveries, learn new ways of working and move closer to the futures to which they aspire. We stay committed to this work because we find that, under the right conditions, such as those Doug presents to us, we can facilitate these types of transformation.

Doug calls this Magic. I agree.

Sandra Janoff, Ph.D.
Co-Director, Future Search Network

WELCOME AND OVERVIEW

Welcome to *Facilitating Transformation: 12 Strategies for Creating Extraordinary Breakthroughs with Groups.* Whether you browse for a few minutes, or dive into each page, I hope you will receive what you are looking for, and perhaps even more. You may gain new insights, or reminders, of how you can generate transformation when you partner with groups.

Here are a few quick questions to get us started:

Who is this book written for?

This book is written for facilitators, teachers, lecturers, trainers, coaches, consultants, and those who work with groups. I am also hoping that others might be drawn to this book as well, and find it useful. After all, these 12 strategies could all be applied to leadership, and the idea of transformation is applicable in many areas of our lives. Therefore, if you have an interest in supporting others to expand their effectiveness, this book could be for you.

My intention is that you extract at least one reminder or insight from each strategy. This nugget of wisdom could be something you already know, or a story or quote might spark a new perspective for you.

Albert Einstein challenged us to "Make everything as simple as possible, but not simpler." The book is simple in some ways, but hopefully not too simple. May your visit through the pages of this book contribute in some ways to the "work" you do.

How to get the most from this book?

Think of this book as a buffet, or a shopping trip. The strategies will taste or look different to you, based on your experiences and perspectives. So sample and try as much as you would like, and take back what is best for you.

This book does not have to be read from cover to cover. The strategies are not a step-by-step formula, but more of a tapestry of possibilities. All the strategies are inter-connected and yet they each can be read on their own. Look around, and take more of what nourishes you and expands your capacity for serving the highest good.

You will probably find it most useful to read the "Introduction" first, to have an idea of what "facilitating transformation" is about. Subsequently, you may want to pick the strategies which are most relevant to your journey as a facilitator. There is also a section at the end of each strategy that offers you some ideas on what you might want to read next. Of course, you can read the book from front to back; the choice is yours.

Another idea of how you can get the most from the book is to consider writing your own story as you read. What would be your strategies and principles for creating successful shifts with the people you work with?

What is meant by "Facilitating"?

To facilitate is to "make easy or less difficult; to help forward or assist in progress". Whether in a formal or informal setting, we have the opportunity to support individuals and groups to make progress towards what is important to them. The objectives could be in areas such as learning, changing, and planning; by facilitating we can make the journey easier and more effective for people and groups.

Why is "Transformation" in the title?

Facilitating "shifts" or "change" could have also worked in the title, but transformation seems to be a higher aspiration. You can call it whatever you like, the idea remains the same, to facilitate in a way that participants and groups gain new perspectives and expand their effectiveness.

Can we always create Transformation?

There is an old joke, "How many psychologists does it take to change a light bulb?" "None, the light bulb needs to want to change itself." Just like the psychologists, we can do our best, but we cannot transform anyone else; we can only create the environment where people and groups make new choices.

There are hundreds of ways we can "be" and things we can "do" to help create the setting for transformation to occur. This book offers you a number of strategies and ideas for being and doing. "How to be?" and "What to do?", those are the questions to ask yourself as you explore the strategies.

What inspired this book?

There were three compelling reasons for me to write this book.

1. I didn't fully realize it at the time, but my foundational experiences as a facilitator were extraordinary. Little did I know that this foundation was preparing me to facilitate sessions with people from all over the world, and in so many different contexts. At some point I began to think it would be good to share what I have learned from these experiences and pass it on to those who might find it useful.
2. I think there is a lot of truth in the old adage that "we teach best what we most need to learn". So writing this book has been transformational for me as well. I feel as if I have climbed halfway up a mountain; I am appreciating and consolidating the journey thus far, and I am also reminded of how far there is yet to travel as a facilitator.
3. For the past few years, whenever I asked myself the question, "If I were to die tonight, would I have any regrets?", my answer was that I would regret not writing this book.

What type of referencing system is used?

All authors and books mentioned in the text are listed in the reference section, along with other books that I find to be relevant and potentially transformational within each strategy.

What terminologies are used in the book?

For ease of reading, there are a few terms which will be used throughout the book:

- "Session" is used to represent a workshop, class, meeting, seminar, lecture, or retreat.
- "Facilitation" can represent teaching, training, lecturing, coaching, or leading.
- "Learning environment" is a classroom, seminar or conference room, or lecture hall.
- "Participant" is an attendee, student, or learning partner.

Is there anything else to know before reading the book?

Each section has examples and stories of how the strategy has come to life. These stories are included to trigger insights or reminders, or to stimulate memories of some of your own stories.

With deep, high, wide wishes and intentions for you to create a transformational experience, may you enJOY the journey.

INTRODUCTION

Education is not the filling of a pail, but the lighting of a fire.
– W.B. Yeats

"Who are you?" asked the caterpillar. "I hardly know sir, just at the present," Alice replied. "I know who I was when I got up this morning, but I think I have changed several times since."
– Lewis Carroll in *Alice in Wonderland*

This introduction sets the context for the 12 strategies that follow. It answers the following three questions:

1. What is Transformation?
2. Why Transformation?
3. What are some organizational and personal examples of Transformation?

What is "Transformation"?

The important thing is this: to be able at any moment to sacrifice what we are for what we could become.
– Charles Du Bos

Transformation is defined as "a change in shape or appearance; to metamorphose; as a caterpillar... to a butterfly". This kind of change represents permanent, enduring change. In the context of working with groups, we explore breakthroughs in mindsets or behaviors–a shift in the way people think, act and interact. Ideally individuals and groups leave the sessions fundamentally different than when they arrived, with expanded ways of thinking and being.

However, even when transformation does not occur during a session, seeds for future transformation are being planted. So, the foundation of this book is based on the belief that we can do a number of things that increase the chances for breakthroughs, both in the session and beyond.

Yes, we can meet objectives, enhance skills, and convey knowledge; we can also create an environment for transformation to occur, for the individuals and groups we partner with.

Are you talking about the "intense, in your face, break you down and build you back up again" kind of transformation?

No, although that is one way to experience transformation. The transformation described in this book is gentle and has more transparency in the process. This way, participants are making conscious choices and empowering themselves. It is then easier for them to replicate their experiences.

What is a simple and practical way to think about "Facilitating Transformation"?

A famous Xerox study, cited in the book *The Service Profit Chain,* offers us a way to think about what transformation is all about. In their customer satisfaction surveys, Xerox used to be satisfied with a customer rating of a "4" or "5", on a 5-point scale. A "3" or below indicated a service recovery opportunity, but "4"s and "5"s were considered good. This makes sense, doesn't it?

But when the researchers from Harvard dug deeper into the Xerox data, they discovered that customers who rated them a "5" were SIX times more likely to renew their service contracts, compared to those who rated them a "4".

The findings of this study present a lesson for us as facilitators. If we expect consistent transformation, excited participants, repeat clients, more referrals, and continued enrollment, then it helps if we are able to deliver "5" sessions. We are not just talking about "5"s on the evaluation sheets ("smiley sheets" are what some people call them), although they are a good start. Beyond that, we are talking about participants having a "5" experience, one that has enduring value and is worthy of sharing with others.

Why "Transformation"?

The simple answer might be "why not?" While there is nothing wrong with incremental change and growth, we can hold an extra intention of creating breakthroughs that can propel us to a new level of being–individually as well as collectively.

One of the foundations of this book is that "transformation" can be an aspiration for every session we facilitate. Here are a few reasons why this is advantageous and helpful:

- Individuals and groups sometimes find it challenging to apply their learning after leaving a session. If they can shift during the session, their transitions and application of learning will be easier.
- We are being asked to help organizations and staff deal with lots of change; the ideas and practice of transformation can expand their capacity to manage change.
- Thought leader Robert Kegan, in his book *In Over Our Heads*, points out that many individuals and organizations are challenged by the complexities of the various contexts they find themselves in. With high intentionality for breakthrough insights, we are able to provide them with ideas, perspectives and skills that transform the manner in which they manage some of these complexities.
- Even when people do not experience major shifts in the session, the seeds of transformation have been planted. It could take months or years before an idea or behavior fully blossoms.
- The sense of satisfaction from being with people and groups as they transform themselves is amazing. Most of us in the facilitating professions engage in this work with a deep sense of purpose, and this gives us the opportunity to engage with others in an even more purposeful way.

What are some examples of "Transformation"?

As mentioned in the Welcome and Overview, stories and examples have been included throughout this book to illustrate the various strategies and concepts. The stories in this introduction chapter are not meant to describe how to facilitate transformation (that is what the 12 strategies are for) but to provide a glimpse of the end results. We will first look at four examples of organization shifts, followed by two examples of personal breakthroughs.

Examples of Organization Transformation

Transforming Business Results

A sales and service center in the U.S. was ranked last out of 23 centers across the country.

Although they had an excellent center manager and competent leaders on the team, they were not able to create a culture of trust and collaboration that was essential for getting results. During a 2-day session for the leadership team, members engaged in a number of group and one-on-one conversations–open exchanges that transformed the energy and dramatically increased trust. In less than six months, the center ranked in the top three of all 23 centers in the areas of both sales and service.

Ready for the Competition

A Singapore organization was facing a business challenge from a powerful global competitor about to make its entry into the local market. The leadership team knew that they had to respond to this challenge. Together, we designed an intensive 3-day experience, filled with open, honest assessments that shifted their thinking. This gathering became a turning point, and allowed the organization to maintain its dominance in the market.

A Transformational Merger

The Asia Senior Leadership Team of a newly merged global organization came together for a 3-day session. From the beginning, it was apparent that the cultures of the two companies were quite different, but this was not being openly discussed. On the first day of the session, the group engaged in a process which allowed them to share their perceptions of their own company culture and business models, and that of the "other" company. Each team showed off their own flaws in ways that was more extreme than the other side could have imagined. This collective "owning up" created high levels of trust with the new team members, and built new possibilities in how they could work together. After they completed talking about the past, they moved on to dialogue on the future they wanted to co-create, and came up with strategies to move ahead. That new organization achieved much higher profits and morale in Asia than in any other region in the world.

Going Global

The Chief Executive Officer (CEO) of a Singapore firm had a vision that the organization could be more global. However, it was not a vision shared by many others in the company. Over two days of intensive activities and authentic dialogue, 30 senior leaders explored the possibilities and payoffs of global expansion. When we left the room, there was little doubt among them that their firm would be a global brand. Today, they have a thriving business all over Asia, the Middle East and Europe.

The aforementioned stories are examples of what successful transformation might look like for teams and organizations. Would those results have been achieved without the workshops? We will never know for sure, but we can do our best to bring about these types of breakthroughs when we work with groups.

While we are not able to guarantee transformation, we can increase the possibility of such shifts. That is the essence of this book; the 12 strategies present a menu of philosophies and methodologies we can adopt to enhance the likelihood of such shifts.

As we intend for organization breakthroughs, we are also intending and creating possibilities for individuals to experience shifts. The following examples are stories of personal transformations.

Examples of Personal Transformation

Personal Leadership

An Asia Pacific leadership team of a large Australian company came together in Malaysia. They participated in a number of discussions and activities, one of which was related to quality issues.

The participants were challenged to perform their own quality control, to manage the integrity of the event. After the activity, one of the leaders shared that he felt terrible about not having called out the quality mistakes. He even expressed that he felt he had failed as a person and as a leader. With heartfelt emotion, he declared: "Leadership is Standing Up for What You Believe is Right." This statement was mentioned repeatedly throughout the session, ended up in company publications, and is still referenced to this day.

The leader adopted "speaking up for what's right" as his personal mission. The session seemed to catapult his effectiveness as a leader to higher levels, and he was promoted twice in the few years following that workshop.

A Mom's Transformation

After introducing a model of personal change to a group, one participant connected deeply with its core message: to hold on to your dreams, especially if they are meaningful and persistent.

The participant was a woman who had given up on many of her dreams. She was working full-time, raising her children, and had few other pursuits in her life. However, after the session, she found the time to enroll in a part-time degree course, took up social dancing, and got involved in community work. Initially, her children thought that she was too old to be doing so many things. But over time they became very proud of her and what she has accomplished. She is now a role model as she supports them in pursuing their own dreams.

What happened in these examples of personal transformation? Well, these participants were probably ready for a breakthrough in their life. The safe environment, engaging facilitation style, and purposeful design supported them to reflect, explore, and shift.

The shifts described in the organization and personal transformation stories are exceptional examples, but they present a picture of what is possible. The idea for this book emerged from years of experiencing these types of shifts on a regular basis; this prompted me to attempt to understand the underlying principles of these breakthroughs.

As we move through the 12 strategies, more stories will follow. Each group and situation requires different ingredients for breakthroughs, so we can be as purposeful and mindful about supporting organizations and individuals to go over their own transformation "tipping point".

Summary

What is Transformation? Transformation is a fundamental shift in how we experience life. When we partner with groups, we can plant seeds for these types of shift to occur, seeds that will blossom in a session, or perhaps in the future.

Why Transformation? In this world that seems to be getting more fast-paced and complex, breakthroughs and shifts are becoming more important for organizations and individuals. Transformation helps people and organizations to be better to deal with change and complexity. If they can create breakthroughs during the session itself, it helps to ensure that the shifts will be sustainable.

We concluded the "Introduction" with examples of organization and personal transformation. These stories are meant to provide a flavour of what breakthroughs might look like, and to remind us of what is possible every time we are with a group.

Some people change when they see the light,
others when they feel the heat.
– Caroline Schoeder

Reflection Questions

- Do you make transformation an aspiration for every session you facilitate?
- How often have the sessions you facilitate achieved a "5" (on a 5-point scale)?

Insights and Expansions

What did you find most interesting about the introduction?

____

____

How can you build your capacity to facilitate transformation?

____

____

Where to go from here?

Now that we have a clearer understanding of what transformation looks like in the context of our journey together, it is time to explore how to make it happen. For that, you might want to start at the beginning, with Strategy 1 "Be Intentional". Or you could also start at the end of the book and read Strategy 12 "Bring Your Whole Self To Work". Otherwise, you might want to check out the table of contents and see if any of the strategies call out to you.

Strategy 1

BE INTENTIONAL

A good intention clothes itself with sudden power.
– Ralph Waldo Emerson

I may not have gone where I intended to go,
but I think I have ended up where I intended to be.
– Douglas Adams

This book is about meeting learning outcomes in a way that creates transformational shifts. This begins with intentionality. Being intentional means having our heart and mind aligned with what is possible in the sessions we facilitate. Intentions are both practical as well as magical: practical because they help us to focus on objectives and aspirations, magical in the sense that some of what is manifested is difficult to explain.

In this strategy, we will explore how intentionality can support us in our work with groups, how to share the power of intentions with others, and then how to use it in our lives. We will conclude this strategy with a contingency intention, as well as some thoughts on the paradox of intentions.

Objectives Are Not Always Enough

Having spent years being intentional (or at least doing my best to remember this practical, magical way of being), I had taken for granted that others would be aware of the power of intentions, especially trainers and facilitators. However, in a few sessions with other facilitators, it became clear that this was not always the case.

> *The greatest danger for most of us is not that our aim is too high and we miss it, but that it is too low and we reach it.*
> – Michelangelo

Most people assume that if you facilitate a session and meet all of the objectives, this would be a success. Well, the following story illustrates some distinctions between objectives and intentions, and offers some ideas on what we can do differently.

Objectives Met and Still Disappointed–Why?

During the train-the-trainer sessions that I lead, an individual or group is invited to facilitate an activity or process. Before the practice session, the person or group shares their objectives. After the activity or process is completed, we debrief how it went.

I became fascinated by the number of times the facilitators felt they had met their objectives, and yet were not satisfied with how things went. I would ask them what was missing. Typical responses were:

- "We wanted the group to enjoy the process more."
- "We were hoping the group would be more involved and participative."
- "We thought the insights from the group could have been more profound."

Over time, it became clear that the objectives were not comprehensive enough. I later asked the facilitators to ensure that their objectives had included what they really wanted for the session. This single change created a significant shift in the outcomes, and became a catalyst in developing the first strategy in this book: "Be Intentional".

The previous story demonstrates the importance of being clear with what we aspire to co-create with participants. In the above example, the facilitators were only sharing their objectives and intentions for one short activity. Imagine how the impact would be magnified over an entire session.

In our work as consultants and facilitators, there are often many more applications of intentionality. Let's take a look at some opportunities to apply the power of intentionality.

Opportunities for Being Intentional

When it comes to being intentional, there are a number of contexts in which we could ask the question "What are our intentions?" Some of them include:

1. Entry/planning meetings–How can we set the stage for extraordinary learning experiences, and model what we would like to see in the upcoming session(s)?
2. Design–How can we design a session that is for the highest good of all?
3. Overall session–What might transformation look like and sound like when the session is completed?
4. Each day–What are the themes and our aspirations for the day?
5. Each module/segment/activity–What insights or breakthroughs can emerge from each part of a session?
6. The group as a whole–How might the group be different than before the session, in how they work together and in the type of organization they co-create?
7. Each participant–What shifts might occur in terms of how they perceive themselves, their colleagues, their work, and their lives?
8. Ourselves–How might we be transformed from the interaction with the participants and the content?

The more specific we are when we think about and visualize what transformation might look like, the more likely it will happen.

Leveraging Our Intentions

How can we help our intentions come to life?

First of all, it helps if we are clear about what is possible, visualizing a future where the intentions are already happening. However, we do not want to limit our intentions only to what we can imagine; so in addition, we can have an intention that even more amazing breakthroughs will occur beyond our wildest imagination.

In addition, it would appear that the qualities of joy, gratitude, and patience are high-leverage states for intentions to come to life. Joy and gratitude allow us to appreciate what is happening in the present, while patience creates the space for the intentions to manifest in the future.

Are intentions guaranteed to happen? No, but the intentionality creates clarity and momentum, which are the practical and magical aspects of this strategy.

At this point, you might be wondering what some of these intentions might sound like. As you look through the list in the following section, see which ones resonate with your highest aspirations for the work you do with groups.

Examples of Intentionality in Facilitation

When we facilitate a session, we usually have objectives and outcomes. Oftentimes, the stated objectives can be a bit clinical, almost like a session to-do list. There is nothing wrong with this, but as passionate change agents, we would often like to generate more than that. The following list is an example of some transformational intentions, all of which begin with "Our/My intention is that...":

- our/my thoughts, words, and actions serve the highest good of all.
- participants realize that they have many choices in how they live their life and create meaningful work.
- participants realize that they are resilient and capable of handling all kinds of situations, regardless of their environment.

- participants appreciate and see how magnificent they already are and how they can joyfully expand their magnificence.
- participants return home after the session and apply their lessons with their family and friends.
- participants will create a common language that will be helpful for their long-term success.
- the group discovers ways to achieve results and their mission in ways they could not have previously imagined.
- the group creates an outrageously fun time as they learn.
- the session is so practical and inspiring that participants will encourage their colleagues and friends to attend future sessions.
- the group creates new and expansive ways of working together.
- participants build partnerships at the session which will enrich their lives.
- participants expand their capacity for qualities such as appreciation, open-mindedness, assertiveness, forgiveness, creativity, love, gentleness, firmness, paradoxes, and change.
- participants realize that they are not alone when they encounter challenges and that support is always available.

> *When you follow your bliss you put yourself on a kind of track that has been there all the while, waiting for you, and the life you ought to be living is the one you are living.*
> – Joseph Campbell

Which of these intentions resonate with you? What are some of your intentions when you facilitate? Can you see that you may not be able to put some of these items in the official course objectives? If you can, it would be even better, because you can get the group to share these intentions.

Group Sharing in Intentions

Besides asking people to share their aspirations and intentions with one another, a simple way for people to experience the power of intentions is when they split up into random pairs or small groups, using count-offs or card sorting. I say something like "If you would like to join me, you can say an intention that you will be with the 'perfect' partner or team for the next part of the session."

Be realistic. Plan for a miracle.
– Osho

One piece of evidence, not proof, that intentions manifest themselves in reality is the numerous occasions participants have approached me during breaks to share miraculous stories about who they ended up with as a partner. For example, once in a conference session with about 30 participants, two people who had been contacting each other via email for years in a professional capacity, but had never met, ended up being partners. That is what is possible when the group joins in with their intentions.

There are numerous ways to involve the group in intention-setting. It could be in the form of asking the group some simple questions, such as "Are you ready to create transformation together?" or "Are you open to the possibility that you can create new ways of doing things you have never even considered before?" It could also be individuals or members in groups sharing with one another their deepest and highest aspirations of what they can co-create in the session.

Not only can we involve people in intention-setting in sessions, we can also remind them of the power of intention-setting in all aspects of their lives.

Being Intentional as a Way of Life

A number of people and organizations do not seem to fully tap into the power of intentions, so it is an idea worth sharing with others. The following is a typical way I introduce the concept to a group:

What Do You Really Want?

On occasion, I share with groups how people and organizations can get caught up in routines and forget to connect with their intentions/aspirations. As an example of this, I mention how couples planning their wedding are often so busy with the guest list, the music, the flowers, etc. that they lose sight of bigger questions, like what kind of wedding or marriage they would like to create together.

In one session, there happened to be a couple in the group who was getting married to each other in about three weeks, providing the perfect opportunity to test the level of intentionality in their planning. In front of their colleagues, I asked them both: "What kind of wedding do you want to have?" After a brief pause, the woman answered: "I want it to be memorable." "I want it to be fun," the man said.

I then asked: "So you are three weeks away from your big day, do you think your wedding will be memorable and fun?" The couple shook their heads, indicating "no".

Over lunch, we brainstormed ways the wedding could be memorable and fun, but the bigger lesson was how easy it is to get lost in the details of life. Intentions and aspirations can be powerful energizers for enlightened action, but only when we remember to connect to them.

Wedding planning is just one example of how we can miss the bigger picture. Can you think of any dimensions in your life where your aspirations have gotten lost in the middle of your to-do list?

My wife Christy and I do our best to be intentional in our daily living. We ask ourselves aspirational and intentional questions. "What do we want to do today?" becomes "What kind of day do we want to co-create today?"; "What's for dinner?" shifts to "What kind of evening would we like to experience?" As you can imagine, a change in the question leads to a different set of answers that often creates an expanded outcome. This does not always happen, but it does occur often enough to appreciate these bigger questions.

Expect the best.
Prepare for the worst.
– Muhammad Ali Jinnah

Now that we have explored the power of intentions and big questions in our lives, we are going to return to facilitation for one more level of intentionality.

Creating an Extra Intention–a "Go" Button for Challenging Days

Since transformation is our aspiration, we want to be able to facilitate extraordinary breakthroughs, even when we are not feeling our best. The next story illustrates a process for creating an extra dimension of intentionality.

Developing a "Go" Button for an Extra Boost of Intentionality

When I was training to be a facilitator, our teacher knew that there would be times when we would be emotionally, physically and mentally exhausted. He was aware that we would be on the road 75% of the time, and facilitating intensive workshops six days a week.

To help us remain great on those challenging days, he asked us to develop a "Go" button, which would serve as inspiration in our work, even on days when we weren't feeling our best. This represented an extra level of intentionality, in addition to the intentions we have for each session, day and module.

I had coached youth sports for more than a decade and my passion was to facilitate confidence and resilience in children. So my "Go" button, which I still access on occasion, is to remember that many participants in sessions I facilitate are parents, who will extend their learning to nurturing confidence, resilience, and other life skills with their children.

This extra intention can help sustain us and keep us anchored, even on the most challenging days.

What is your "Go" button?

We can see that intentions can be held in various contexts, and that we can even have a contingency intention, an anchor, on days when we need an extra boost.

Brewing Tea and Intentions

Nothing happens but first a dream.
– Carl Sandburg

There seems to be a paradoxical quality about intentions. Just as "a watched pot never boils", the likelihood of brewing a transformation seems to decrease if our intention is that transformation *must* happen. When boiling water for tea, most people find it best to turn on the stove and patiently keep an ear out for the whistle to signal the water is boiled, while doing other things. If it seems like a long time and there is no signal that the water has boiled, then it would be a good idea to go back and take a look at the stove and see what is happening.

Similarly, it seems best to state our intentions and then joyously facilitate, while we patiently keep an ear out for the intentions to manifest themselves. If we do not notice any of the intentions occurring, it is good to revisit them and see what is going on. A group might prefer coffee instead of tea, and the intentions can be shifted.

So our intentions are meant to be strong and clear, yet with a light sense of attachment. Best wishes in finding the most elegant balance with your intentions.

Summary

When we have the intention for transformation, we align our hearts and minds in visualizing what might occur. Intentions are both practical and magical, and are a good place to begin to plant the seeds for transformation. We can plant these seeds in meetings, activities, sessions, participants, and groups.

They can be planted in many areas of life, and are usually best fertilized with a combination of clarity, openness, joy, and patience.

Being intentional can become a way of life, by checking in with questions such as "What do I/we want?" or "What would be for the highest good in this situation?" We also looked at developing contingency intentions for more challenging times, and were reminded to hold intentions with a light touch.

Our institutions are transformed the moment
we decide they are ours to create.
– Peter Block

Reflection Questions

1. Do you make transformation your goal before engaging with a group: for each module/activity, for each person, as well as for the group and the session as a whole?
2. What are your highest intentions and aspirations for the "work" you do?
3. What is your "Go" button when you are struggling, either physically, emotionally or mentally?

Insights and Expansions

What did you find most interesting about this strategy?

____

____

How can you build your capacity to Be Intentional?

____

____

Where to go from here?

If you are reading this book from cover to cover, you know where to go next. If you would like to forge a unique reading path, you can roll a pair of dice and allow its outcome to guide you to your next strategy for reading. As you are about to roll the dice, hold the intention that the number on the dice will direct you to the strategy most suited for your learning journey.

Strategy 2

BE PRESENT WITH PRESENCE

For the spiritual warrior, every moment
is a challenge to be genuine, and each challenge is delightful.
– Chogyam Trunga Rinpcoche

What time is it? NOW. Where are we? HERE.
– Dan Millman

Being present, as a facilitator, refers to staying present to the purpose of the session, the individuals, and the group, as well as to the environment and our intuition.

Presence is attained when we are centered and grounded, and when we focus our intentions and attention on what is happening in the group.

We will begin our exploration of how this strategy emerged, and how this lesson of being present saved me from possible injuries. We will then look at a few stories which illustrate what being present might look like and one where it was missing in action. We will conclude with two specific areas of being present and purposeful, spending time with participants during breaks and meals, and being aware of defining moments of transformation.

Whether it is clear to you or not, no doubt the universe is unfolding as it should.
– Max Ehrmann

How This Strategy Came About

The following is the story of how I learned the power of being present. I was fortunate to learn this lesson early in my life as a facilitator–within the first week of working with groups.

Learning to Be Present by Falling Down

I was about to make my first ever appearance as a facilitator in a session. The energy in the room was high and at the last minute, I had an idea to trip myself deliberately on my way to the front of the room. Spontaneously, I hooked my feet against the leg of a chair and landed flat on my face, in front of about 60 participants.

There was a collective gasp in the room, but I picked myself up and confessed that I was only joking. The group burst into laughter and we spent the rest of the session having fun, while exploring ways to create miracles together at AT&T.

The session ended on Saturday, and a new group arrived on Monday morning. After what had happened the week before, I thought my fake fall would be a great way to break the ice again. So I tripped myself again as I moved to the front of the room. When I got up and told the group that the fall was intentional, the group stared at me in silence with a look that read: "Do you actually think that a cheap trick like that would make us laugh?"

Fortunately, I had three days to recover from this embarrassing start.

On hindsight, I have immense appreciation for that experience for at least three reasons:

1. I became aware that each group, like each individual, is different. Since that fateful fall, I started to do my best to dance to the rhythm of each group I am with. Each group is like a friend or a dance partner whom I want to get to know better.

2. I learned, and continue to learn, that there seems to be a fine but distinct line between doing things intuitively, and doing things as a technique. There is a certain power that comes with feeling connected to the group and the environment, and trusting our intuition. This feeling helps us know what we can do for the highest good of the group, in that moment.
3. I'm sure I would have injured myself at some point with all the falling, so I am thankful to have saved myself a trip to a hospital emergency room.

Being present is a gift we give to the people we work with and to ourselves, and it is a way of life. A few years ago, I attended a concert which deepened my appreciation about being present with a group.

Tuning In to an Audience, with Presence

Bobby McFerrin, best known for his song "Don't Worry, Be Happy", was in Singapore to perform a concert a few years ago. When he was introduced, he shared that he went on stage without planning what he was going to sing. Instead, he tunes in to the audience and relies on a higher wisdom to guide him towards his next song. The evening had a magical feeling to it, being in the presence of such presence.

> *Live in the present, launch yourself on every wave, find your eternity in each moment.*
> – Henry David Thoreau

Another source of inspiration from Bobby McFerrin can be when things go off-track in a session; we can sing "Don't Worry, Be Happy" to ourselves as we reflect on how we can best serve the group at that point in time.

As important as it is to be present and go with the flow with a group, we also have content and process to honor as well. Herein lies the challenge: how do we achieve the best of both worlds? How can we dance to the tune of the group, yet deliver the content in a way that serves the group's highest learning?

Staying Present with Presence in Extraordinary Circumstances

To bring out the essence of this strategy, the following story provides an example of being present with a group, balancing what was happening in the room with the content that was planned for the session.

Let's Take a Timeout and Talk

In March 2003, I was in the midst of facilitating a session with a global team from the World Bank, when someone announced that the U.S. invasion of Iraq had begun. Upon hearing the news, a participant, whose son was a U.S. soldier stationed in Iraq, stood up and said that he was returning to his hotel room to keep track of the latest news, while others made side comments that they felt this was a senseless act of aggression on the part of the U.S.

Within moments, the atmosphere in the room grew tense and it became clear that this issue was more important than our session objectives, at least for that moment. I asked the participants whether they would like to continue with the session or to stop and talk about what was happening in Iraq.

There was a general consensus to talk about the war. Everyone was given the opportunity to take a microphone and share their feelings, but not their opinions, about what was happening. For about 30 minutes, people shared a full range of emotions with the large group. Eventually, one participant made what felt like the perfect integrating statement; he summarized all the sharing and invited everyone to send their loving thoughts and prayers to the citizens and soldiers in Iraq. We took a moment of silence, followed by a short break, and then resumed with the planned session.

The feedback from participants indicated that they appreciated the flexibility of the session, were inspired by the authenticity of their peers, and benefited from the learning process before and after this sharing session.

While the event described above was an extraordinary situation, it provides a reminder of how we maintain a delicate balance between the design of a session and staying present to the needs of the participants.

However, it does not take a dramatic event to take us away from the design of a session. For example, the participants could become engaged in a stimulating discussion on an important topic that is not on the agenda. This is a valid reason to consider altering the plan.

While the World Bank story above is a positive example of being present with a group, there have been a number of occasions where I lost track of this simple strategy–the phrase "easier said than done" comes to mind.

Caught Up in the Content

There are a number of distractions which could take us off-track. There are time constraints, the contents of the course, or even personal matters that are on our mind. It is also possible that we allow ourselves to become distracted by the behavior of certain participants, or by some of the group dynamics.

The next story illustrates an occasion where I was so focused on the content of a session that the participants became overwhelmed and exhausted.

An Overloaded Afternoon

I facilitated a half-day session for a group of change agents, sharing and practicing a number of engagement processes, as part of a 3-day workshop.

I was eager to impart as many processes as possible within the short time frame, as I wanted the participants to have a full range of tools in their change agent toolbox. When the participants started to display signs of tiredness and lethargy, part of me knew that it was time for a break, but I ignored the thought.

The feedback at the end of the day from the participants was that they felt there was an overload of processes and information, and that the afternoon session was not very effective. For me, the external signs and internal thoughts were to stop and check-in, but I didn't do it. So this was another reminder to pay attention and to take action.

The above encounter serves as yet another reminder to "Be Present". In addition, it is also a reminder of how challenging it can be to be an agent of transformation, when we are not tuned in to the participants or surroundings.

Being Present to You, in the Here and Now

Since we are immersed in the spirit of being in the now, here is my attempt to guess what you are thinking. I am guessing that it is one of the two following thoughts:

1. That you would never make the mistake mentioned in the previous story. (Fair enough.)
2. That it is unrealistic for anyone to be 100% present. (I agree.)

Of course, there is a third possibility, that you are thinking about something different, such as an email you read a few minutes ago. But even if I am wrong, that's ok. We may never be perfectly aware, but we can do our best to be conscious of what is happening around us. We may not always know what to say or do, but it is a vast improvement over going through the motions or pushing our agenda too hard.

The following story demonstrates this dilemma in action, and shows how changing our internal question, and trusting intuition, can create a shift.

Team Transformation–from yes to NO to YES!

Some of the sessions I have facilitated included outdoor adventure learning. Once, I was with a group of about 15 people for an afternoon (one of four such groups) who had a low level of energy and participation. I did everything I could to engage them in the activities but nothing seemed to work. The scorching hot Singapore afternoon probably caused some of their fatigue, but all the other groups were doing ok.

It seemed like it was going to take a miracle to salvage the day. So I changed my internal question from "How can I get them to do the activities?"

to "What does this group need right now?" The answer I received on this second question was to ask the group if they wanted to continue the activities or go back to the hotel. This was not a logical approach, but the voice in my head was clear and so I offered the group the choice. They shouted: "Yes, let's go back to the hotel for some air conditioning and rest."

While we were making our way back to the hotel, one of the participants commented that they were missing out on the activities and it seemed absurd that they were giving up so easily. Almost miraculously, the other participants echoed similar sentiments and everyone agreed to return to the field to rejoin the activities. When we returned to the site, the energy of the group became incredibly high. They began cheering and screaming words of encouragement to each other. This group became one of the loudest and most passionate groups I have ever been with. They transformed their level of teamwork and support and took a new spirit back to their work together.

Was this decision risky? Yes, especially given the fact that there were three other teams still out in the field. Was that the only way to facilitate transformation? Probably not. Have I ever done this again? No. However, on that day if I had continued to push the participants into following my agenda, they would probably have gone through with the program and not experienced any major shifts. But that magical question "What's most important now with this group?" opened up more possibilities.

From this experience, two significant lessons emerged:

1. To regularly ask myself the question, "What's Important Now (W.I.N.)?", and to be with the question and allow intuition to flow. Over time, this becomes more a way of life in addition to being a question to ask when facilitating.
2. That offering others the choice to say *no* gives them the opportunity to make genuine choices.

The lessons thus far in this "Be Present with Presence" strategy have been focused on group facilitation. However, breakthroughs can occur in other contexts as well, not just from the front of the room.

Getting Immersed–Another Way of Being Present

I learned about another dimension of being present in one of the first sessions I was part of, with two colleagues from AT&T.

Our teacher, Horst Abraham, was there to observe and mentor us. While we were busy with the final preparations, Horst playfully told us that he was probably going to make more of a difference in the session than we were. We were surprised to hear this, as he was just going to be in the background, not in front of the room at all.

Presence is more than just being there.
– Malcolm Forbes

When we asked him to elaborate, he told us that we would be occupied with the practical aspects of the session, such as the logistics, charts, as well as reviewing our flow, content, and instructions. However, he would have the opportunity to build connections with participants during the breaks and meal times.

While we were preparing for the next module, he would immerse himself in transformational discussions with participants.

This lesson struck a chord in me, and to this day I do my best to remember that transformation can take place anywhere, not just from the front of the room.

Whenever I partner with other facilitators, we make it a point to huddle up at breaks and meals to do a quick "check-in"; we then split up and spend our lunch and tea breaks with different clusters of participants. It could be to gather feedback about the session, to see what questions they have, or to explore the ideas they find interesting. As Amy Tan, a fellow colleague at AT&T, always says at the end of our team huddles, "Let's get immersed!"

Whether we are talking with one person or a group over lunch, or facilitating a small group debrief, it helps to remember that breakthrough opportunities can show up in an instant.

Magic in the Moment

Sometimes what is happening in a session gives us an opening to explore real-life patterns for the individuals and groups we are with. These can often be defining moments of transformation.

> *You can observe a lot by watching.*
> – Yogi Berra

For example, imagine a person says in a soft voice, "My goal is to be more assertive". That statement made in such a mild manner is an opportunity for some exploration. One option is to ask if others are working on being more assertive, and for them to brainstorm together as a group. Also, there may be participants in the room who could offer some advice. Another option is to ask what assertiveness would sound or look like for that person.

Group dynamics often show up in ways worth probing. Some issues that can be noticed, brought up, and discussed in sessions include: how groups make decisions, the quality of conversations and listening, the type of humor group members use, certain team members being marginalized, etc.

Workshops are a bit like a reality TV show. We may only get a glimpse of what happens behind the scenes, but from time to time, we get to witness events that represent a bigger story, a pattern of behaviors. Here is an example of when an event in a session mirrored real life at the office and provided a good source for some transformation lessons for the team:

Team Dynamics

I recently facilitated a session in which a team was challenged to complete a systems thinking challenge. The leader of the team quickly solved the challenge and explained the answer to the team.

I didn't think that the team members understood his explanation, but nothing was said. When I asked, it was confirmed that no one understood exactly how the problem had been solved. He explained it again, and then he asked if he was clearer this time. They then talked it through until everyone understood both the logic and the solution.

This was a simple workshop activity, but was it representative of a larger pattern of behavior that happens at the office? It turns out the answer was yes. The team then engaged in a dialogue about how the leader could check in more often on the level of understanding of business issues, and the group members could make more effort to clarify issues that were not clear. While still not perfect, they are making strides at the office to increase the collective intelligence of the team.

By being present with presence, and looking for such "in the moment" observations, we can help participants see themselves more clearly. This can trigger meaningful reflections and discussions, and thus create shifts in mental models or behaviors.

Let's take a quick look at "presence" before completing this strategy.

The Power of Presence

When we are present with a group, and feeling centered and grounded, the group will sense our "presence". Think about the occasions when you were with people who were present to you, with a strong presence. It is a powerful experience.

The most precious gift we can give others is our presence. When mindfulness embraces others, they will bloom like flowers.
– Thich Nhat Hahn

I remember sessions when I felt connected to 100 or more people, when I could sense what was happening in the room, almost with each person. I do my best to create these moments by being clear on intentions, focusing my attention on each person AND the entire group, and taking some deep breaths as the session progresses.

Summary

Being present with a group means to be aware of the balance between sticking to the plan and being spontaneous, and to sense what is best for the highest good of the group.

A question we can regularly ask ourselves to help us be more present is "What's Important Now (W.I.N.)?" This question can help maintain our focus and in the spirit of transformation. We have also looked at how we can facilitate shifts even when we are not in front of the room, by being immersed with participants during breaks and meals. We proceeded to look out for real- life issues playing out in a session, those defining moments that can help create significant breakthroughs.

When we do all of the above and are able to be grounded and centered, then our ability to connect with the group is enhanced. Best wishes to you in being present with presence in the groups that you work with.

Create each day anew.
– Morihei Ueshiba, Aikido O'Sensei

Reflection Questions

1. How are you at being present in sessions; focusing your attention and intention with groups and individuals?
2. Are you consistently tuning in to groups, to sense "What's Important Now (W.I.N.)?"
3. Are you willing to immerse yourself with participants during tea breaks, lunches and other free times, in meaningful ways?

Insights and Expansions

What did you find most interesting about this strategy?

How can you build your capacity to Be Present with Presence?

Where to go from here?

To find out which strategy is best for you to read next, you could tune in to the here and now and allow your inner voice to guide you.

Strategy 3

GO FOR 100%

The openness of our hearts and minds can be measured by how wide we draw the circle of who we call family.
– Mother Theresa

If you reach for the stars, you might not quite get one, but you won't end up with a handful of mud, either.
– Leo Burnett

There is a saying in many parts of the world, something like "you can't please everyone"; this saying seems to have become an unspoken truth in the world of facilitation as well. While we are not in the business of "pleasing people", there are numerous advantages to finding ways to facilitate in a manner that every participant chooses to get involved in the learning process.

When all participants are involved in the learning process, the group's energy and sharing is like a ride on an upward spiral. This is beneficial for the individuals as well as the group. We will examine how to create the conditions where each participant sees value in engaging in the session.

With this goal in mind, this strategy intends to deepen our understanding on how to reach out to 100% of the participants, and develops our appreciation for the skepticism in a group (note the word *skepticism*, rather than labeling someone a skeptic).

How This Strategy Came About

There seems to be a concern that if we focus our attention on the few participants who do not seem engaged in the learning process, we risk the session going off-track and alienating those who are interested in learning.

Earlier in my career in facilitation, this dilemma was real for me as well. Do I focus on the 80%–90% who seem genuine about learning, or the 10%–20% who have their arms folded and do not seem interested in being "here"? Well, I have since discovered that we don't need to make that choice; we can make it our goal to reach out to every participant, bearing in mind that we do not just deliver content, but also aspire to co-create transformation.

The following is a two-part story that conveys how this "who to focus on?" dilemma was transformed into the strategy of "Go for 100%."

Learning to Go for 100%

It was the final afternoon of a 3-day session in St. Louis. During the last tea break, I was looking around the room for someone to talk with. I realized that I had made a meaningful connection with every participant, except one. I was thinking of talking to him, but decided against it, as he seemed rather unapproachable, being the strong and silent type. I spoke with someone else instead.

After the session ended, I began reviewing the evaluation forms for feedback tips. Imagine my surprise when I came across the form from the strong and silent guy, and the improvement tip for me read "Could be more approachable and friendly when not in front of the class."

As I read this, I had a flash of insight–that my impression of him mirrored his impression of me. From that moment on, I committed myself to approach those seemingly unapproachable participants at the first opportunity.

~

I was living out this new philosophy, when an opportunity presented itself about two months later, in the Washington DC area. While another facilitator was presenting the course introduction, a participant started playing his Sony Walkman so loud that everyone in the room could hear it. Not only was the noise from the Walkman disruptive, the tall and fierce-looking participant even yelled a few obscenities, and told everyone not to listen to the company brainwashing.

At the first available break, I approached him and asked how he was doing. He replied that he was doing better than usual, knowing that he would be out of the office for three days. I asked if there was anything we could do to help make the session valuable for him. Upon hearing the request, he seemed to relax a little and expressed that he had nothing personal against us and would do his best to cooperate.

Later that day, we found out why this gentleman was so upset. He was HIV-positive, his partner had just died from AIDS, and he felt that the company was not sympathetic of his situation. Over time, his bosses became less tolerant of his absence from work, and as a result, he became even more rebellious. Eventually, his colleagues lost faith in him and avoided associating with him as well.

During the three days, he gradually opened up to everyone. By the third day, he became the group cheerleader and re-established his relationships with his colleagues. This "transformation" continued when they went back to the office.

This experience had a lasting impact on me. It helped me to realize that the powerful energy of resistance has the capacity to morph into high levels of transformation.

While the workshop was transformational for this gentleman, it was also a significant shift for the other participants and the organization. So when the 10%–20% choose to get engaged in the process, it benefits the larger system as well.

I feel fortunate to have received so many lessons in such a clear manner. Triggered by the feedback from a participant, I developed a philosophy of reaching out to others, which was validated a short time later. That was how the "Go for 100%" strategy originated.

When we commit ourselves to reach out to 100% of the participants, we become more aware of what is happening in the room, more mindful of the language we use, and more purposeful in designing a session with each participant in mind.

Different Folks Need Different Strokes

Having committed ourselves to the 100%, what do we do next? Well, in certain cultures and groups, it is easier to spot the people to talk to, as they are open about their opinions and concerns. In other cultures and groups it is more difficult to identify those who are not enjoying the learning experience. They could be smiling and seemingly agreeable to everything, but they may be struggling in the session. So talking openly and directly may be a good idea for participants who are more outspoken, but it may be counter-productive for others, unless sufficient trust has been built.

This philosophy of reaching out to 100% takes into consideration that we do not know the circumstances of every participant. Participants who appear resistant have their own story to tell. Perhaps they have been forced to attend the session, or simply do not believe that an intervention of this nature will make a positive difference. It could be that the participants are not at all resistant, but are just tired, or their arms are folded because they feel more comfortable that way, or even that their face appears strained because of indigestion.

Transformation with the "Dilberts"

When we do not attempt to reach out to 100%, we risk invalidating the learning experience for the other participants.

I have heard of sessions which were considered unsuccessful because the facilitator conducted the session in a way which inspired only the participants who were already inspired (some people call it "preaching to the choir"). The participants who were more skeptical, or more discerning, later convinced the "inspired" staff that the ideas presented were not applicable in their work context.

Therefore, it is important to consider the opinions of everyone in the session and organization when we facilitate with transformation as our goal.

For a number of years, I worked in the Information Technology (IT) field, a profession which has spawned a lot of "Dilberts". For those of you who are not familiar with him, Dilbert is a fictitious comic strip character developed by Scott Adams. He is an engineer who will not be winning any awards for "Employee of the Month". And even if he did win it, he would surely reject it or do something outrageous with the prize. Dilbert has a sense of humor that speaks to the cynical part of anyone who has ever worked in the corporate world. Can you recognize any Dilberts in your life, or part of him in yourself?

> *Everything that irritates us about others can lead us to an understanding of ourselves.*
> – Carl Jung

I have worked with a number of "Dilberts", especially in IT, and I have traces of him in me as well. This is not necessarily a bad thing, as a healthy amount of skepticism ensures that we are capable of doing practical work. If we are able to reach out to the "Dilberts", the participants who are seemingly the most cynical, they can become the biggest supporters of the work we are doing together. When preparing for a session, I ask myself if Dilbert would enjoy and benefit from the process. If the answer is yes, I know things will turn out well.

You might be thinking that it is impossible to reach out to everyone. That may or may not be true, but what a wonderful aspiration to bring to a group of people. Even when not everyone chooses to engage in the learning process, we will be a better person for trying, and will learn something in the process. Also, we will be planting seeds for future transformation. Here is a story where the seeds were planted, and later blossomed:

Do Our Best and Trust the Process

I was facilitating a 2-day leadership and business development session for a Leadership Team. Everyone seemed to be engaged in the process, with the exception of one participant. This participant disagreed with much of what was being discussed and sat cross-armed for most of the session.

I approached this participant during a break and asked how things were going. He said that the session was fine. I did not feel comfortable with this answer and asked: "I am wondering if I can make any adjustments to what we are doing or to my facilitation style?" He thanked me for asking and then said that there was nothing I could do, since my approach seemed to be working well for everyone else.

When the session came to an end, I felt that 19 out of the 20 participants left feeling very satisfied, with this one exception. Although I felt disappointed, I knew I had done my best.

Much to my surprise, I received a call from that client a couple of months later with a request to design and facilitate a series of sessions for that particular participant's department–the very person whom I did not think appreciated the workshop. He wanted me to work with his department. He subsequently told me that he appreciated my willingness to approach him openly and directly, and was impressed by how much his colleagues had benefited from the session. We partnered on a few projects and he was a delight to work with.

Looking back, I think this came about as a result of the commitment to reach out to 100% of the participants, instead of settling for just 95%. This is just one of many examples which illustrates the power of going for 100%.

As in the previous story, the seeds of transformation are often not obvious at first, but sometimes sprout when we least expect them to. Of course, there are times when a participant does not benefit from a session and we never hear from them again. Nevertheless, it helps to know that we have done our best to provide a meaningful learning experience for every participant.

Creatively Reaching Out to 100%

When we commit ourselves to this 100% goal, we will find creative ways to facilitate. The following story is one such example, where creative engagement of a participant helped to create shifts for a group.

Partnering with Skepticism

On the first morning of a 3-day leadership session in Singapore, all the participants were on their feet for a visioning activity, with the exception of one leader, John. I asked him if he was willing to participate with the rest, and he said no. I told him that he could choose his level of participation, and asked if he was willing to share with everyone the reason for not wanting to participate in the activity.

John told everyone that leadership sessions were not practical, and were a waste of time. He was only here because his boss made him attend. I then asked the other participants if they ever felt skeptical about the practicality of leadership workshops. Everyone agreed that this thought had crossed their minds.

I then asked John if he would be willing to be our reality check–if he would assess the practicality of each idea and activity throughout the session. He took on this role, and shared his thoughts over the three days. He did not participate in any of the group activities, but he was engaged in his own way.

John became a great spokesperson for the collective skepticism in the group, and we were all privileged that he was willing to speak out and share his insights.

A few months later, John and I had a chance encounter on the streets and had a short chat. He told me that he managed to take away some ideas from the session that had helped him be a better leader. And I shared my appreciation of his willingness to be our reality check–to ensure we were engaged in meaningful and practical work.

As in the above story, engaging skepticism might be a first step leading to transformational experiences. Peter Block, author and consultant, does his best to engage the cynical part of an organization. During the contracting phase of an intervention, he asks, "What concerns do you have about what we are going to do?" If they claim to have no concerns, he follows up with, "If you did have any concerns, what would they be?"

All Opinions Are Valid–Engaging 100%

The first few stories in this strategy described conversations with participants that happened over a tea break. The most recent story illustrated a situation where the conversation took place with the entire group. Both methodologies can be useful and effective, depending on the situation.

If it depends on the situation, then what are the considerations? Well, there is a simple guideline to follow. If we are not sure how a participant is feeling about the session, then it is best to have a one-on-one chat to see how they are doing.

However, if a participant openly states an opinion, or refuses to engage in the process, this is an opportunity to engage the person AND the group to create a more complete picture of reality, and to create an opportunity for a breakthrough.

How do we manage a situation in which a participant challenges an issue in the session or states a strong opinion which is out of the norm?

We start by being present to the person, bearing in mind that all opinions are valid. We have at least four choices:

1. We can clarify the meaning they are trying to convey.
2. We can open the discussion to the group and gather more opinions.
3. We can explain our perspective to the person and see if that addresses the issue.
4. We can do sub-grouping. In sub-grouping, we ask who else agrees with the opinion stated by the person, and who has a different opinion. We canvass the entire group to see how many opinions there are and ask everyone to vote

on the opinion they feel most aligned to. If participants do not feel aligned to any opinion, they can start their own sub-group. Then each sub-group talks among themselves about their own opinions, to build understanding within and between the sub-groups. Each sub-group is given time to share their thoughts, without responses from other sub-groups. After all the sub-groups have expressed their opinions, the dialogue opens up to the entire group, until someone makes an integrating statement.

All of these options are effective, depending on the situation. Hopefully we are present enough with a group to know which one to choose.

The sub-grouping option, the fourth of the choices above, is the least common way of facilitating disagreement, but the one that is most likely to engage 100% of the participants.

The goal of sub-grouping is not to spark a debate, but to get 100% of the group involved, to build a more complex and complete picture of reality, and to allow integrated, enlightened perspectives to emerge from the group.

To learn more about sub-grouping, you can read *Don't Just Do Something, Stand There* by Marvin Weisbord and Sandra Janoff. Here is an example of sub-grouping in action:

Sub-Grouping–Engaging 100% in an Emergent Dialogue

I was with a regional leadership team from a global organization to facilitate change management, as they were about to merge with another large company. As we began the session, one leader asked why we were spending half a day on change management, when they were all experienced in leading change.

I asked if others felt the same way, and two raised their hands. I asked who had a differing view, and the rest indicated that they were looking forward to this half-day session. After each sub-group had a good chat among themselves in front of the entire group, the discussion opened up to the entire group.

After a few comments, someone said that this was the first time they were going through a merger as a team, and suggested that they use this session to leverage on their lessons from the past, so as to ensure a smooth transition. This idea was enthusiastically supported by everyone in the room–including those who had initially expressed reservations.

Not only was 100% of the group engaged in the discussion, the level of energy in the room shifted to a higher level.

Forming sub-groups allows for everyone to register and express their opinions, and feel that their voice is heard and honored.

Whether we go for 100% in a one-on-one discussion or with the entire group, our aspiration remains consistent; we want to create an environment where everyone chooses to be part of the learning process.

One way to ensure that we are creating a "100%" environment is to be aware of what participants might be thinking, and to show that we understand their considerations.

Sensing and Anticipating Participants Thoughts

In every group, there will be participants who have a higher level of skepticism and cynicism. Even in the most optimistic individual, there would still be some cynicism. If we become aware of this in ourselves and in the group, it can increase the chances of transformation, because we will have more choices on how to address the cynicism.

Part of being able to reach out to 100% of the participants is being able to sense and anticipate objections to what is being done and said in the session. Here are a few examples:

- If you know that some participants may have done a particular activity or process before, ask the group "Have any of you done this before?" If there are participants who respond with a "yes", let them know how it might be different this time, or ask them to share advice for the others who are doing it for the first time.

- If you hear yourself saying something that might not be 100% true, you can qualify the statement. For instance, at the end of some sessions, I ask participants to write a letter to themselves, one that will be mailed back to them in a month or so. I instruct them to seal the envelope and assure them that no one else will read the contents. But since there is a possibility that someone else might read the letter, I then add "At least no one will read it unless you show it to them."
- Imagine you have just introduced some ideas to a group, and you are sensing that some participants do not find them to be practical. You could say "I sense that some of you might need some time to warm up to these ideas. But take your time to digest the ideas, and try them out for yourself in a low-risk situation and see how it turns out for you. What questions do you have?"
- If we think there are participants who are well-versed in the content, we can tell a story about martial artists. Martial artists learn most of the techniques they need to learn in their first year of practice, but their practice can continue for a lifetime. If they are not learning new techniques, what are they learning? It might be speed, elegance, ability to handle more complex situations, etc., and then maybe to become teachers. So this story helps those who are already proficient in the content of the session to see the possibilities of doing things faster, smoother, in more complex situations, and to help facilitate learning for others.

Whether we are working with a group of six or 6,000 participants, we can anticipate what the participants might be thinking, when there is an exception in something we say. By anticipating these thoughts, we can address their concerns, without the need for anyone to voice them out. Or at least we can try.

Feedback for Future 100%

In order to keep reaching out to 100% in future sessions, it helps if we are able to receive feedback from all participants (See Strategy 11 "Seek And Celebrate Feedback"). It is easy for a facilitator to focus on positive feedback from participants, and to lose track of those who did not have a transformational experience.

Imagine a participant approaches us after a session and says, "Wow, that was a fabulous session and it has changed my life. Thanks so much." This sort of comment validates the wonderful work we do.

However, if we are not careful, we might overlook the feedback from the participants who did not enjoy or benefit from the session. Those participants usually pack up quietly at the end of the session and leave the room. Evaluation forms do not always tell the complete story either, as some participants might not feel motivated to provide any feedback. It takes effort to find out how we could improve our capability to reach the 100%.

Best wishes to you in creating and facilitating sessions that every participant will experience as useful and impactful.

Summary

To "Go for 100%" refers to committing ourselves to being intentional and present, with each and all of the participants in sessions. We have explored how it is possible to focus on both the inspired learners as well as those who appear resistant. We then become more purposeful when designing a session with every participant in mind, more aware of what is happening in the room, and more mindful of engaging the skepticism in the room.

In this strategy, we considered the distinction between participants who are more outspoken and those who are more reserved, and also whether or not to address participant concerns over a break or in front of the group. We also explored the available options in dealing with apprehension in the room with sub-grouping, which maximizes engagement and learning.

One final reminder in this strategy was to be mindful of the quality of the feedback we receive from participants. Getting high quality feedback from participants builds our capacity to reach out to more people in more effective ways in the future.

Every object, every being, is a jar full of delight.
Be a connoisseur.
– Rumi

Reflection Questions

1. How are you at accepting and honoring everyone who shows up in the sessions you facilitate, and in your life?
2. How are you at approaching participants who seem resistant and not engaged in the learning process?
3. Would Dilbert enjoy your sessions and benefit from them?

Insights and Expansions

What did you find most interesting about this strategy?

____

____

How can you build your capacity to Go for 100% ?

____

____

Where to go from here?

Besides proceeding in sequence to Strategy 4 "Tune In and Engage", you can consider other options. Perhaps you would like to explore Strategy 11 "Seek And Celebrate Feedback", to ensure that you are doing all you can to reach 100% in future sessions. You could also read about the role language plays in reaching out to 100%, in Strategy 7 "Mind Your Language". To focus on appreciating and connecting with all participants, you can check out Strategy 9 "Be A Transformer".

Strategy 4

TUNE IN AND ENGAGE

Many children struggle in school...
because the way they are being taught
is incompatible with the way they learn.
– Peter Senge

If the only tool you have is a hammer,
then you tend to see every problem as a nail.
– Abraham Maslow

In this strategy, we will explore the diversity of learning styles we encounter. We can be intentional that we will provide a range of experiences which allows participants to learn in a way that maximizes their chances of transformational shifts.

After a story on adding a learning modality in the midst of a session, we will tune in to Confucius for some thoughts on learning. We will proceed to examine a number of frameworks, each one offering a unique twist of the kaleidoscope of learning modalities. This strategy will close with two examples of activities that engage people in a variety of ways. If you are an experienced facilitator, you may want to skim the section on the frameworks, and see if the activities are useful for you.

Let's begin by looking at tuning in to the frequencies of the participants we engage with, in this wonderfully diverse world we live in.

Tuning In to the Participants

Do unto others as they would like to be done unto.
– The New Golden Rule, for Learning and Communication

What is your favorite radio station? If you can answer this question, then you have found a radio station that is on a similar frequency as you. However, not everyone listens to the same radio station, and many people have more than one favorite station. Others do not listen to the radio at all.

This metaphor of radio stations is analogous to engaging participants in sessions. After all, each participant has their favorite stations and frequencies, demonstrating the diversity of the people we meet, and their varied styles and preferences. Our challenge and opportunity is to tune in to the frequencies of the participants, to play a combination of learning modalities that create a transformational learning environment.

Using a variety of engagement methods is important, and requires intentionality and presence. Even when our mix of methods is not perfect, we can always adjust, as in the following example:

Transformational Singing

I was facilitating a 4-day session in Taiwan, with the leadership teams of three operations in the country. We were reinforcing the vision, mission, and values of the organization, as well as engaging in some Leadership and Team Development.

On the second day of the session, I became concerned, as the participants seemed reserved. The activities in the session would typically have created more energy and engagement. Although the participants said that the session was excellent, I sensed there was something I could be doing differently.

It was my first time facilitating in Taiwan, so I asked around to find out how people liked to learn. The responses seemed to suggest that they were not sure how they like to learn, but indicated that they enjoyed singing. Participants told me that in Taiwan many business deals are done in karaoke sessions. In fact, many people engaged voice coaches to help them improve their singing skills.

So at the next opportunity, I asked groups to write and perform songs that captured the spirit of the organization. During the 30–40 minutes of composing and singing, the energy and the creativity of the interactions and discussions shifted to a higher level, and stayed there for the remainder of the session. In this elevated state, the group was able to gain more clarity on the organization they wanted to create, as well as the strategies to make it happen.

Because singing was so engaging for this group, we concluded the 4-day session with a song. We sang a beautiful Chinese song (Jacky Cheung's *Zhu Fu* for those of you who know Chinese music) and almost everyone was in tears by the end of the song.

This story shows the importance of being flexible in the modalities we utilize to facilitate engagement. It is also a reminder to try to understand the learning preferences of the participants in advance. Either way, it is helpful for us to have a number of learning modalities in mind as we design and facilitate a session.

Confucius and Learning Modalities

"I hear and I forget. I see and I remember. I do and I understand." You may be familiar with this quote by Confucius, as it is often cited for the reason to learn by doing. I think Confucius would be impressed by the numerous ways of learning that are encouraged in classrooms and sessions in the world today, and I think he would be ok with some telling and showing, as long as it was of a high-quality.

However, he might also be puzzled by the number of participants who are still disengaged or bored in sessions they attend. Here is a question for you: "Are participants and students stimulated in the sessions you facilitate and teach?"

If the answer is a clear "Yes", then head to another strategy, or just do a quick browse of this strategy to see if all the models are familiar to you. If the answer is "No" or "Not sure", then explore each of the frameworks in the next section, and see which ones serve as useful reminders for you.

Because we are intentional about reaching out to 100% of the participants, let's commit ourselves to create experiences where each person's learning preference is part of the process. This increases the chances for breakthrough insights, for individuals as well as groups. Thanks to Confucius for encouraging teachers to get learners more involved, and for planting the seeds for us to discover multiple ways of learning.

Engagement with Multiple Modalities

To make our lives easier for remembering modalities/frequencies, there are a number of frameworks available to use as a reference. Over the next few pages we are going to explore a few of such frameworks: Neuro-Linguistic Programming (NLP), the Learning Cycle, Multiple Intelligences, and Spiral Dynamics.

For each framework, there are ideas on how to engage the participants belonging to the modalities. Some of these might be familiar to you; others might be new. Either way, read, listen, feel, play with, and reflect on the frameworks and identify the ones that you find most useful.

We begin our journey with a framework from NLP. This practical model is a popular and useful way of engaging participants in the learning process (Figure 4-1).

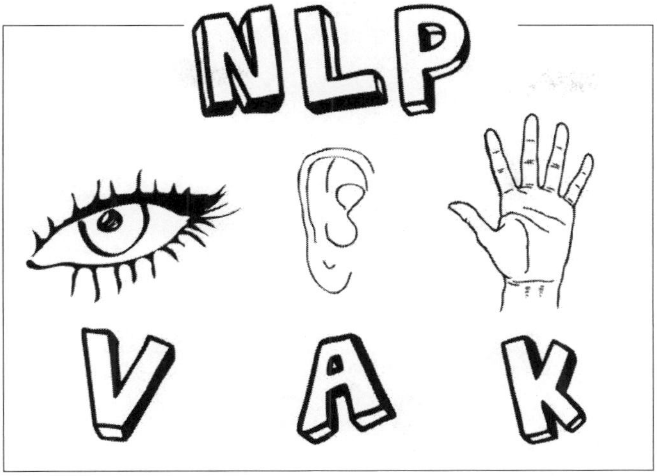

MODALITY	SOME IDEAS FOR ENGAGING PARTICIPANTS
Visual	Use posters, videos, stimulating slides and materials, drawings, and flipchart creations.
Auditory	Be sure to vary the tone and volume of your voice. Also allow the learners to share their ideas and listen to each other. Play music.
Kinesthetic	Get people involved physically, to provide lessons at a cellular level in the body. You can engage in activities, shift seating arrangements, dance, and provide opportunities for movement.

Figure 4-1: NLP framework

How do you like the NLP framework? You might want to do a quick analysis on your application of the three NLP modalities. How are you at engaging participants in visual, auditory, and kinesthetic ways?

Next, we move on to David Kolb's Learning Cycle and Learning Styles. This is an excellent model for designing engagement for maximum application of learning (Figure 4-2).

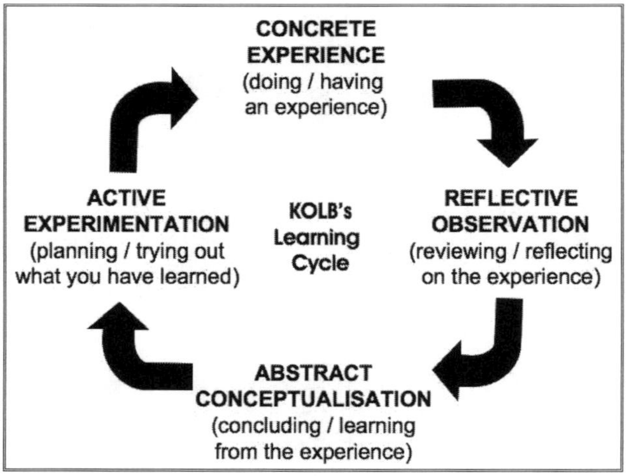

STAGE OF LEARNING CYCLE	SOME IDEAS FOR ENGAGING PARTICIPANTS
Concrete Experience "Doing"	Provide experiences through activities, discussions, role plays, etc., anything which has the potential to stimulate reactions.
Reflective Observation "Reflecting"	Provide participants with the chance to reflect on what has happened, or to analyze the experience.
Abstract Conceptualization "Generalizing"	Explore systems, theories, concepts, or models. Make connections between events and theories. Let people develop theories of what is the difference between success and failure in certain situations.
Active Experimentation "Experimenting"	Engage in activities and share stories which are practical and applicable to everyday life. Work on real issues and make time for action planning.

Figure 4-2: Kolb's Learning Cycle

Can you see the power of this learning cycle and the learning styles? A session designed around this cycle will provide engagement which can produce insightful observations, new theories, and innovative solutions.

The third framework in this strategy is the Theory of Multiple Intelligences, developed by Howard Gardner. This is a comprehensive framework for tuning in and engaging. These intelligences, along with some ways to bring each one into a session, are represented in Figure 4-3 below:

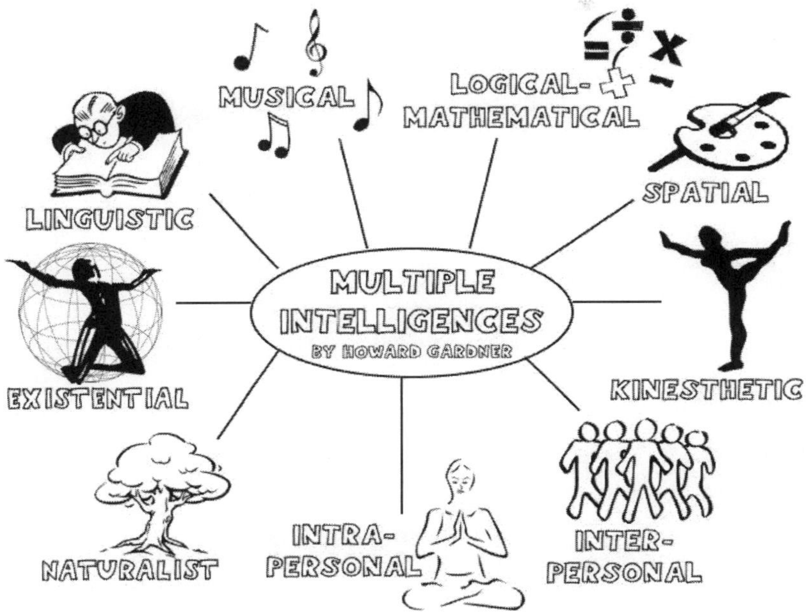

INTELLIGENCE	SOME IDEAS FOR ENGAGING PARTICIPANTS
Linguistic	Use clear language, the language that the participants can relate to. Be sensitive to language levels in the session, especially if the language you are using in the session is not the native tongue of some participants.
Musical	Play music. Be conscious of our voice tones and modulation. It may even be helpful for participants to design and sing songs based on the theme of the session.

Figure 4-3: Theory of Multiple Intelligences *(continued)*

Logical-Mathematical	Ensure that the session has enough structure and logic, so that there are minimal distractions from the learning process. Let the participants know why certain things are being done, so they can relax and learn.
Spatial	Give the participants the chance to present the concepts, or their learning in creative ways. They can draw or take pictures, or use existing pictures to illustrate points. A bonus to this type of learning is that hidden skills often surface.
Interpersonal	Allow for interaction between participants, to share ideas, lessons, experiences and stories. Often people learn more from each other than they do from us facilitators, or the content.
Intrapersonal	Give the participants the opportunity to reflect. This can be done through journaling, asking reflective questions, or giving them the chance to gather their thoughts and meaning along the way.
Kinesthetic	Involve participants in movement. This could be through activities, gestalt representations of concepts, or even performances.
Naturalist	Create connections to nature, and perhaps even spend some time in a natural environment. This could influence the choice of venue to hold the session.
Existential	Put the session in a larger context. Explain why the context and exploration are important.

Figure 4-3: Theory of Multiple Intelligences *(continued)*

Professor Gardner believes that everybody possesses all intelligences, but in varying degrees. In the type of sessions that you teach or facilitate, how can you engage these intelligences in a way that maximizes individual and collective learning? A bonus of introducing more intelligences into a session is that it allows hidden talents to emerge in a group, in areas such as art and music.

One last framework for our engagement exploration is Spiral Dynamics, originally the work of Clare Graves, and further developed by Chris Cowan and Don Beck. Spiral Dynamics is a model which represents developmental stages, worldviews that influence how we experience life. The spiral system is summarized in Figure 4-4 below:

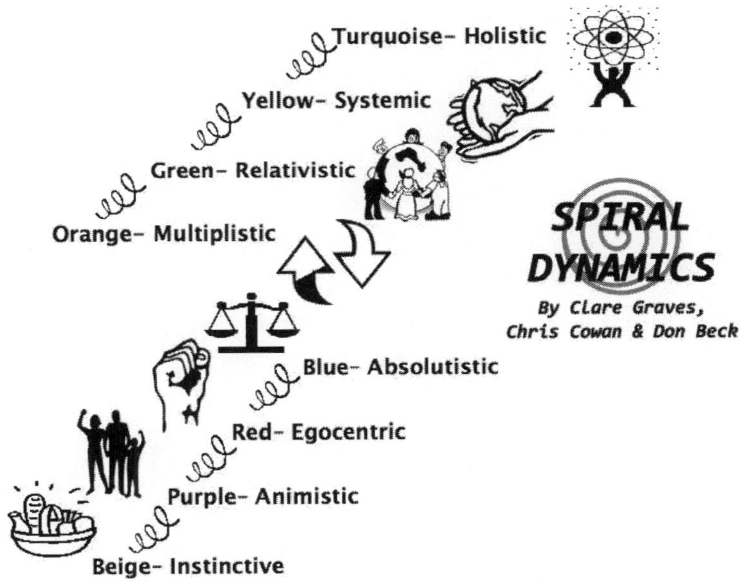

WORLDVIEW	SOME IDEAS FOR ENGAGING PARTICIPANTS
Beige-Instinctive, *Focus on basic needs*	Be sure that everyone's basic needs are taken care of: food, drink, comfort.
Purple–Animistic, *Focus on community*	Create opportunities for the group members to experience a sense of community, do rituals together, and be able to support each other.
Red–Egocentric, *Focus on power and expression*	Give participants the chance to express themselves, and provide choices for participants to make along the way.

Figure 4-4: Spiral Dynamics *(continued)*

Blue-Absolutistic, *Focus on rule and discipline*	Ensure that the session has structure and an agenda. Implement some guidelines in the process, like being on time after breaks. Show how we can become better human beings and a better community from the process.
Orange-Multiplistic, *Focus on change and progress*	Help participants to see that they can make things better, to change, to improve things, to create more excellence and success.
Green-Relativistic, *Focus on equality, diversity & the environment*	Make connections to help participants see how to create a more sustainable and equitable world.
Yellow-Systemic, *Focus on the entire system*	Give a big picture perspective, work together to build individual and organizational capacity.
Turquoise-Holistic, *Focus on the inter-connectedness of all life*	Dialogue on the inter-connectedness of life and how can we live for the highest good of all species on the planet.

Figure 4-4: Spiral Dynamics *(continued)*

This model supports a spectrum of human development. What is your impression of the Spiral Dynamics framework, and can you provide participants with a full range of experiences and perspectives?

This range of models is meant to give you an idea of what type of frameworks you could use to tune in and engage with the participants, not that you need to make sure that every preference of every model is employed. There are numerous other frameworks as well; for example, a simple model could be to consider the main dimensions of human beingness: mental, emotional, physical, and spiritual.

Also, most personality profiles provide practical frameworks for being strategic about engaging each and all of the participants. An added bonus of personality profiles is that you can create engagement at the personal, interpersonal, team, and organizational levels.

Which models are most helpful to you, as you think about designing and facilitating a session?

If it is difficult to decide on which one(s) to use, here is a creative idea. I have heard of facilitators who start their sessions with a short learning styles assessment. After tallying the assessment, the facilitator engages the group in a discussion about the learning styles in the group. Together they redesign the session, adjusting the learning modalities to the overall preferences of the group, and also the learning preferences of those in the minority groups of learning styles. I have never used this approach, but find it interesting and thought you might enjoy the stimulation of this idea.

Two Engaging Activities

Now that we have explored a number of frequencies to tune in to, here are two examples of activities that engage participants in various ways of learning, with a number of the aforementioned frequencies.

Snapshots–a Multi-Modality Learning Experience

Snapshots is a versatile and engaging activity. Small groups (6–10 in a group, and with up to about 10 groups) are given a digital camera, with instructions to take pictures that represent the theme of the session. This could be the future of the school or organization, their values or mission, or of an opportunity or challenge they are facing.

The groups are invited to leave the room and even the building, to explore the surrounding area, and to take creative pictures that represent the theme. Upon returning to the room, each group is given a photo printer, flipchart paper and some markers to create a storyline or collage, with captions of their photos. Each group then presents to the large group, followed by an open discussion.

The charts and presentations then become the focal point of the rest of the session, to provide the launching pad for exploration and action.

Often the masterpieces on the charts will make their way to the offices, hallways, and pantries back at the organization, to serve as a reminder of what transpired at the workshop.

From the above, you can see that the "Snapshots" activity engages participants in a wide range of learning modalities.

Let's look at another activity that engages learners. One frequency that seems to tune in to learners around the world is when they are working on issues that are important to them. The following process is adapted from a process called Action Learning, and modified for a workshop setting.

Engagement Through Action Learning

This multi-dimensional activity can be conducted with hundreds of people, arranged in groups of 4-5, formed with as much diversity as possible. The activity engages small groups in issues which are transformational in nature.

Each person takes their turn to share a big opportunity or challenge they are facing in their work: something that if achieved, could transform their business or organization. When one member shares, the other group members act as consultants. However, they are only allowed to ask questions for the first 10–15 minutes of the consultation, before opening it up for dialogue and learning summaries.

Through this activity, group members often have breakthrough insights on their issues, based on the questions from the other members or from the open dialogue.

These breakthroughs emerge from the total engagement of group members. They are addressing important issues, challenging themselves to ask powerful questions, learning more about what is happening in other functions or organizations, and focusing on ideas that could contribute to their expanded success.

This Action Learning process, as shown above, is simple and allows for many possible breakthrough opportunities.

The "Snapshot" and "Action Learning" activities represent examples of engaging participants in ways that plant the seeds of transformation.

Summary

Using multiple modalities engages participants more deeply in the learning process, which becomes a strong foundation for transformation. We have explored a number of frameworks we can keep in our facilitator toolkit for reference, and looked at two activities that engage people and groups in multi-dimensional ways. Let's continue to tune in to participant's learning frequencies and maximize transformational possibilities.

I don't believe people are looking for the meaning of life as much as they are looking for the experience of being alive.
–Joseph Campbell

Reflection Questions

1. What are your favorite frameworks for designing and facilitating for maximum engagement?
2. How flexible are you in making adjustments to the learning modalities you use, based on the learning needs of groups you are with?
3. How often do you engage participants in multi-dimensional activities?

Insights and Expansions

What did you find most interesting about this strategy?

____

____

How can you build your capacity to Tune in and Engage?

____

____

Where to go from here?

In some ways, this strategy serves as a foundation for the next one, "Design for Transformation". If you are not moved to go there, you can tune in and engage someone nearby; ask them to pick a number from 1 to 12 and let that decide your next strategy.

Strategy 5

DESIGN FOR TRANSFORMATION

Every organization is perfectly designed to get the results it is getting.
– Tom Northup

Strictly speaking, there are no enlightened people,
there is only enlightened activity.
– Suzuki Roshi

Much of the success of any session is determined in the design phase. The difference between a good and transformational session is often marked by the choices we make in the processes and activities we incorporate into the design of a session.

In this strategy, we will look at some guiding questions for design, ones that support us to inquire into the potential for breakthrough insights. We will look at the design phase from three perspectives: firstly, the individual elements; secondly, how the individual elements fit together; and finally, an exploration of some "Large Group Interventions". These large group engagement processes offer templates and principles, with transformation already in the design.

Guiding Questions for Design

Let's assume that the objectives and intentions of a session are clear. It's time to sit down and design the session, with the main question being:

> *"How can we design this activity, this process, and this overall session in a way that creates the greatest possibility for individual and collective transformation?"*

As we answer this question, it helps if we have some ideas on what those transformational shifts might look like. We are also open to be surprised with breakthroughs we never could have imagined.

If we are confident that we are about to facilitate a transformational session, that is a good sign. However, if we are uncertain, we can continue to ask ourselves what we can do differently. We may or may not get a breakthrough answer, but we can allow the question to percolate and see what emerges. After all, we do not need to be perfect, but we can strive for perfection.

There are a number of specific questions to ask in designing a session. Some of them include:

1. To what degree will the participants be challenged to reflect and take ownership of their learning and outcomes?
2. Do the participants have a number of choice points along the way? For example, will they be given the opportunity to be open and authentic with their peers, to be courageous in speaking out for what they believe in, or to choose their level of participation?
3. How many opportunities are there for the participants to challenge, support and learn from one another?
4. Are the activities and processes relevant to how the participants live and work, and will they get the opportunity to work on their most pressing issues?

Additional design questions, depending on the context of the engagement, come from the work of Marvin Weisbord and Sandra Janoff:

- If transforming a "system" is the objective, are the "right people" coming to the session?
- If this is a multiple day session, can it be designed in a way that leaves the participants with big questions to "sleep on"?

A moment's insight is sometimes worth a life's experience.
– Oliver Wendell Holmes

These guiding questions can help us meet objectives with a transformational approach. Another consideration worth pondering is how much we, as facilitators, believe in the processes and activities we facilitate.

Facilitator Passion for an Activity or Process

When a facilitator believes in the transformational power of an activity, or process, magic seems to occur at a much higher rate. The same activity conducted in an identical manner can produce different results, depending on the facilitator's belief in the activity. Hence, if you are scheduled to facilitate an activity or process that you do not believe in, try to find your passion for it; explore the possibilities for breakthroughs that may occur. Otherwise, get a co-facilitator to conduct that segment, or consider the possibility of a re-design.

The following is an example of a team activity that I did not use for years because I couldn't find my passion for it. One day I had an "aha" about the activity, and have since used it effectively on a number of occasions.

Transforming an Activity

The "Blindfold Square" has been a popular activity in team sessions. The basic version of the activity is to blindfold the participants and challenge them to work together, to find a large rope and form a shape, such as a square (hence the name "Blindfold Square"). There are a number of variations to this activity, but hopefully you get the idea.

I had observed this activity a few times, but did not feel that it had much transformation potential in it. There were some lessons about communication and listening, but nothing seemed particularly insightful. Perhaps a more skillful facilitator could have generated transformation out of this, but I did not feel confident about doing so. Since my philosophy is not to use an activity unless there is at least some potential for transformation, I did not use it.

However, one day I had an idea to modify this activity and make it more transformational. Here is the variation: before the activity, I identify some participants who are more reserved. Then, while the team is locating the rope, I remove the blindfolds from these quieter team members. I tell these "un-blindfolded" participants that they are allowed to say whatever they want and can ask questions, but they are not to reveal that they can see, or imply it in any way. I explain that this is a challenge for them, to speak up when they possess additional information, and to observe if the team listens to them.

This twist in the activity has a direct application to life in organizations, where many people have additional information about customers, technology, etc. The question is whether the organization is able to benefit from these insights, particularly from quieter people, or those lower in the hierarchy. This activity has produced an incredible amount of personal and group transformation, with rich discussions about corporate culture and group decision-making.

For example, a military team was engaged in this activity in which one of the civilian staff who was "un-blindfolded" shared an idea, but was told to "SHUT UP" by one of the Colonels because he was the leader. Later, when the Colonel found out she could see and was merely trying to help, he apologized profusely. This group then engaged in an insightful debrief about how they could work and communicate together.

The debriefs of this activity have been consistently impactful, because of the real-life parallels it offers. Some quieter individuals do not share valuable information with the team, and the more vocal or higher level staff often do not listen when they do speak up; hence the team does not leverage on its collective intelligence.

The variation of the activity in this story was a result of a commitment to only use activities that offer potential for major insights.

You may be of the opinion that some activities are not meant to create transformation. An activity may be done just for fun or to help participants get better acquainted; for example, some activities are designed with the intention to help participants warm up for more meaningful discussions later in the session.

Even when fun is the objective, we can still ask the question: "Is there anything we can do to make this transformational?" Here is an example of how a simple getting acquainted activity can be modified to create higher levels of engagement and to plant seeds for breakthroughs.

Reflections, Intentions, Ownership and Engagement–Planting Four Seeds for Transformation in a Simple Debrief

Imagine an opening activity of a conference or session where participants get to interact with one another, doing something as simple as introducing themselves to people they don't know very well. There are a number of ways to make even this simple activity more meaningful. Here are the instructions for one such possibility, by debriefing the activity in a way that provides reflections, connections, and insights:

Verbal instructions: "Before you sit down, find someone you don't know very well and sit together." After everyone settles down with their partner, or in small groups, then continue: "This session offers you an opportunity to learn new things, and to build relationships with people here. You are the one who will make your time here valuable, maybe even transformational. So now you are going to have a chance to reflect on the quality of the relationships that you have built in this opening activity, share some intentions, and learn how you can support each other."

The following instructions are then explained, and shown on a slide or chart:

1. Share with each other how you feel about the quality of the connections you made during the opening activity.
2. What type of learning and what kind of connections/relationships will make this session a valuable investment of your time and energy?
3. What do you need to do in order to maximize your learning experiences while you are here?
4. How can you support each other to reach your aspirations for the session?

This debrief creates the opportunity for participants to:

1. start reflecting on their behaviors,
2. set and share their intentions,
3. take more ownership of their learning outcomes, and
4. build a supportive learning community.

Once again, the above example is the product of the question: "Is there a way to make this activity more meaningful and engaging?"

At this juncture, it would be ideal if we could jump out of the pages of this book to share ideas on how we can increase the transformational qualities of the activities we use. Perhaps we could meet in person or online sometime and have a chat on this topic.

In the meantime, here is an example of a common process that can be enhanced with an additional element in the design. This has to do with a shift in the way a "360 degree" feedback is processed.

"360 degree" feedback has become a common leadership and organization development tool in many organizations. Often, recipients process their feedback reports with an external or internal coach, and sometimes on their own. An action plan is then developed to address the opportunities that showed up on the report, and to celebrate the strengths of the recipient that appeared.

A transformational twist can be added to this process. The recipients of such feedback can share the findings with their colleagues openly. This process does not require the participants to share specific scores or results, hence, it is a wonderful opportunity for each participant to choose how open and vulnerable they will be when it is their turn to share. When this process is carried out in a safe, trusting environment, both individual and group transformation can take place.

Below is an example where one person shared the feedback she had received, and created shifts for her and for the organization.

Transformational Sharing and Shifts

A Singapore organization of about 4,000 staff had just created a new set of corporate values. The CEO and I met to discuss the design of a facilitated session for the senior leadership team. We thought it could be transformational for the senior leaders to offer peer feedback to one another, on how they were perceived to be living the new values. This would make the values more personal and help them come alive.

Qualitative and quantitative feedback was collected in the morning of the session, and then a few hours were spent exploring ways to make the values come alive within the organization. In the afternoon, each of the 25 leaders was presented with their feedback report, and given time to reflect and to prepare a 2-minute presentation for the entire group. The presentation was to include what they had learned from the feedback, what they will do differently, and requests for support from the rest of the team.

As the presentations began, a few participants shared quite openly and the environment in the room was beginning to shift. Then the COO shared that she was appreciative of the feedback, and was disappointed that she had given others the impression that she was overly task-oriented. She shared that she had scored low in the area of "respect" and had received comments that her emails and interactions were often seen as impersonal.

She did not realize the impact that she had on others, so she apologized and explained that she was merely trying to better manage her time, with so many emails and meetings to attend to every day. She committed to being friendlier in her emails and interactions, especially with colleagues she did not know very well. She followed through on her promise and this shift was much appreciated by her colleagues.

While the COO's personal shift was one type of transformation, the other type was organizational. Once the other team members saw how the COO shared so authentically, it created a safe environment for them to do likewise. It was a memorable afternoon for everyone, and that team operated at a higher level of trust and effectiveness after that day.

If the leaders in the organization were given their reports on their own, these shifts would not have occurred. Once again, the question "How to make this activity/process more meaningful and engaging?" created more possibilities for breakthroughs.

Overall Design–The Whole Can be Greater Than the Sum of the Parts

Thus far, in this strategy of "Design for Transformation", we have explored ways to enhance individual elements of a session. However, there is also the session's overall design to consider.

For individual segments of a session, we asked "How can this segment be made more transformational?" We now ask a similar question directed at the macro level of "How can the whole session design be enhanced to increase the chances of individual and group breakthroughs?"

Transformational design is exemplified in the Leadership Development work at the Center for Creative Leadership (CCL). As part of a typical learning process, leaders are given psychometric instruments, presented with "360 degree" feedback, and given peer feedback, while they participate in meaningful activities and simulations.

With this variety of input, participants get the opportunity to see themselves from many different perspectives. From these multiple viewpoints, they are able to put together a picture of who they are now, and who they aspire to be. While each section of the session presents potential for transformational insights, the largest "aha" usually comes during the integration time spent with a coach.

As an Adjunct Facilitator and Coach with CCL, it is immensely rewarding to consistently see participants experience significant shifts from this purposeful process.

Another example of overall design is to create a session with four levels of exploration: personal mastery, partnerships, teams, and organizations/communities. Each level can contain transformational elements and the process unfolds in a logical way for participants. The design comes full circle when the participants are asked to leverage their personal mastery to help shift the organization or community.

The overall design process seems challenging to describe. However, assuming that many of the individual activities and processes have breakthrough possibilities, here are a few ideas on how to create a transformational design:

- Create a storyline to the journey; for example: Creating a Map, Building Capacity for the Journey, and Moving Ahead. Another possibility is: Completing the Past, Visualizing the Future, Dialoguing Success Strategies.
- With a small team, it is potentially transformational to meet each team member before and after a session, or to alternate between team and individual coaching sessions. This creates a high level of synergy between personal and team development.
- In dealing with topics such as Leadership and Change Management, I find that most people "know" a lot about these topics, but it's the "doing" which is more difficult to carry out. If you are facilitating a session where this is the case, it is helpful to include an activity where participants can experience the "gap" between what they know and what they do.

- If a session design is based on a model, it is ideal to include an activity around each of the elements of the model, followed by an integrating activity.
- Personality profiles often offer interesting possibilities for overall design. Most profiling is done for personal and inter-personal insights. This can be extended out to team dynamics and organization development, as well as stakeholder management.
- Another possibility for personality profiles is to conduct an activity before or after the profiling instrument is described, in which participants see the elements of the profile play out in the dynamics. It can be quite an "aha" when this happens.
- Begin with an activity that can anchor the entire session. The "Snapshots" activity in Strategy 4 "Tune In and Engage" is one example, or the Systems Dynamics "Beer Game" (refer to www.solonline.org/pra/tool/beer.html) would be another.
- End the session with a powerful integrating activity. Center for Creative Leadership's "Visual Explorer" (refer to cclve.blogspot.com) would be one example, as would a round robin of appreciation and lessons learned.
- See if there is a way for the session to be done with two nights as part of the process, which can be three full days, or a half-day, followed by a full-day, and completed with a half-day. There is something magical when people are engaged in intensive reflections, and have two nights of sleep time, or "soak time".

We do our best to put the pieces of a session together to complete a wonderful jigsaw puzzle for transformation. Continuing with the metaphor of the jigsaw puzzle, we are fortunate that there are a number of thought leaders who have already constructed some elegant designs for us. Having looked at individual and overall design, we now move ahead to look at existing designs, with transformation already built into the process.

Large Group Interventions

There are now a growing number of design templates for engaging groups. This is an exciting aspect and a growing trend in the world of facilitation. We now have many choices from a menu of facilitation processes, rather than having to reinvent the wheel for each session we design and facilitate.

> *There is great power in thinking whole system, and in being a whole system as you think.*
> –Roland Sullivan and John Scherer

When Barbara Bunker and Billie Albans wrote "Large Group Interventions" in 1997, they profiled 12 such engagement processes. Today, there are more than 60 design templates to consider, most recently documented in the *Change Handbook*, by Peggy Holman, Tom Devane, and Steve Kady.

These designs provide us with more than just templates, but also include a set of principles and conditions for success. We can then explore a menu of processes and principles, and select the one that best fits the client's objectives and desired outcomes. Also on the menu is the option to mix or blend some of the principles and processes.

Do not worry if you are not yet familiar with some of the engagement processes mentioned in this section. The good news is that there are plenty of resources to guide you on this exploration. To assist you, the reference section at the back of this book contains a list of resources, and you can find a wide variety of useful information on the Internet.

An example of a masterful overall design is "Future Search", by Marvin Weisbord and Sandra Janoff. Besides the process, the "Future Search" principles illustrate how the process creates transformation in many types of organizations, and in diverse cultures around the world.

The Principles of Future Search are:

- Get the "whole system" in the room. Invite a significant cross-section of all parties with a stake in the outcome.
- Explore the "whole elephant" before seeking to fix any part. Get everyone talking about the same world. Think globally, act locally.

- Put common ground and future focus front and center, while treating problems and conflicts as information, not action items.
- Encourage self-management and responsibility for action by participants before, during, and after the future search.

Can you see the transformational possibilities when these principles of "Future Search" are followed?

As mentioned previously, "Future Search" is one of a growing number of facilitation processes that has transformation built into the design. The increased complexity of many organizations, combined with the desire for whole system transformation, has created the conditions for an explosion of possibilities.

What follows is an example of how these large group interventions facilitated transformation in an organization. Here is the story:

Open Space to a New Culture

Recently I partnered with the Strategic Planning Team of a large academic institute. The purpose was to explore the possibility of expanding their annual strategic planning session from the senior team of about 12 people, to a much larger number.

To reach this objective, we met numerous times to dialogue on the processes that might be the most impactful. We eventually decided to begin the strategic planning process with an "Open Space", followed by a series of "World Cafés" a week later.

We chose to start with an "Open Space" because we felt that it had the highest possibility for creating a cultural shift in the school. An "Open Space" begins with a circle, in this case with 150 educators in a ballroom. Individuals are asked to come forth to the middle of the circle, to share their passion with the large group, and post it on the market place agenda.

When the space is "opened", there is sometimes a moment or two of silence before anyone moves. Because the organization culture was conservative, the strategic planning team was concerned that no one would stand up and "open the space". However, there was just enough trust in the participants, the process, and our intentions to take this risk.

After what seemed like 5 minutes (it was probably only about 30 seconds), one of the lecturers stood up and announced the topic that he was passionate about. Once he started, others followed suit. One by one, a number of participants took the microphone and declared the topics they wanted to discuss with others.

What made this process so powerful for the institute was that the lecturer who was the first to "open the space" became a symbol of a new culture at the school. Instead of waiting for the senior leadership team to make decisions, the message was that everyone was a leader. If anyone had an idea they believed would help the students or the school, they could form a team, gather resources, and make it happen.

Schools, similar to many other organizations around the world, have become too complex for a small group of people to know everything needed to expand its effectiveness. A culture of engagement and empowerment can be jumpstarted by one of the large group processes.

This is one example of how breakthroughs can occur with a large number of people. Again, transformation is built into the process, and can be carried out with thousands of people.

The desire to involve more people in planning sessions was uncommon about 20 years ago, and there were not many processes at the time to help accomplish that objective. The desire and the processes have grown hand-in-hand.

Paradox of Perfect Designs

There seems to be a paradox that can happen when our design seems perfectly matched to the group and the objectives of the session. There have been a few sessions in which I was so confident in the design that I unconsciously relaxed on Strategy 1 "Be Intentional" and Strategy 2 "Be Present With Presence".

While these sessions were still effective, they did not seem to have the anticipated magic and transformational impact. As a result, I am more mindful of being intentional and present when I notice that I feel overly confident in the design.

Summary

Session design is an expansive topic. The BIG question we have explored was "How can we make this activity/process/session more transformational?" With this question in mind, we will create new and more elegant, powerful designs. We also looked at how the various elements of a session fit together, to further enhance breakthrough insights.

The final topic of this design strategy was about large group engagement processes. A menu of interventions is available for us to browse and choose from, to find a facilitation process that is best suited for the situation. Each intervention design provides inspiring principles and a process which has already proven effective, at least in certain contexts. What a wonderful time to be involved in facilitation.

Best wishes to you in your design process, in finding the right activities, the overall flow and engagement processes that serve the highest good of the people and groups you partner with.

That is what learning is. You suddenly understand something you'd understood all your life, but in a new way.
– Doris Lessing

Reflection Questions

1. How persistent are you in asking yourself powerful questions as you design a session?
2. How are you at designing high levels of engagement and ownership into the learning processes that you facilitate?
3. Are you familiar with a wide range of engagement processes, and their principles?

Insights and Expansions

What did you find most interesting about this strategy?

____

____

How can you build your capacity to Design for Transformation?

____

____

Where to go from here?

If you would like to know how the design ideas apply to working with teams, you can head over to Strategy 8 "Breakthrough With Teams". Otherwise, you might want to write the numbers 1-12 on small slips of paper. You can close your eyes and pick a slip, which will guide you to the next strategy to read. If you pick the number of a strategy that you have already read, perhaps the strategy has a further insight for you to discover with a quick browse.

Strategy 6

DESIGN THE ENVIRONMENT

The classroom should be an entrance into the world,
not an escape from it.
– John Ciardi

If you give a hungry person a fish, they won't be hungry. If you teach a person to fish, they'll never be hungry. But, if you create conditions within which the person teaches themself to fish, they will never be hungry and will have enhanced self-esteem.
– Will Schutz

As each session is held in a space where transformation is our aspiration, our exploration in this strategy will be how to create a sacred learning venue.

With so many types of sessions and settings, there is no definitive design that can be prescribed to maximize transformational possibilities. Moreover, it is not always possible for a session to be held in an ideal conditions. Nevertheless, we can do our best to be purposeful in designing the environment.

The following pages will take you through some ideas that I (and many others) have found to contribute to transformation in some way. We will look at bright expansive views, table and chair arrangements, music, wall space, visual recording, books, rituals, group empowerment, and energizing the room.

- **A bright space with many windows**

  A spacious room with many windows creates a good foundation for transformation. It seems that expansive views create expansive perspectives.

- **Do not use tables**

  Some of you are probably nodding your heads in agreement with this idea, while others might be thinking "What! No tables?"

  A room without tables creates a higher sense of openness and vulnerability, and thus increases the chance of shifts happening in the session. This arrangement becomes especially helpful and practical when the session requires the participants to move around a lot.

  However, sometimes clients express concern when I request for a room set-up without tables. I have heard everything from "Where will they place their drinks?" to "This is unacceptable in our corporate (or country) culture!" The client usually agrees to give this option a try, and most of the time the organizers and participants get quite comfortable by the end of the session.

- **Use small tables**

  This point might seem contradictory to the previous point, but it offers an alternative when the "do not use tables" option is off the table, so to speak. This could be for a number of reasons, such as having a large amount of training materials, or the need to do a lot of writing.

  Small tables create a sense of intimacy; with four or five people at a table, it makes it easier for everyone to get involved and feel connected. This set-up has been made popular around the globe by the facilitation process, "The World Café".

  If tables are being used, consider setting the table in a way that creates a cozy environment. The tablecloth can be a sheet of flipchart paper, with markers and/or crayons provided for drawing and scribbling. Other ingredients can include sweets and fruits for munching, and a flower as a centerpiece. The idea is to create a space where participants will feel more comfortable, and hence more inclined to engage in the learning process.

- **Be strategic in the chair arrangement**
  A question to ask when preparing a room is "What chair arrangement would be most aligned with the objectives of this session?" The chairs can be arranged in a circle, a semi-circle, or in small clusters of chairs. The next two stories are examples on how the arrangement of the chairs matches the flow and energy of a session.

Examples of Chair Arrangement

Seated in Harmony with the Session

At AT&T, our team travelled the world facilitating a 3-day session called Project Miracles, with groups of about 50 to 80 participants. On the first morning, the chairs would be arranged in structured rows facing the front of the room, with sufficient space in between the chairs to provide everyone with a comfortable distance from the person sitting next to them. Thus, the session would begin with a focus on the content of the workshop, at the front of the room.

Over the course of the next two days, the participants began to take up more ownership of the learning process, and the arrangement of chairs mirrored these dynamics. As the session unfolded, the distance between chairs became smaller, and the chairs were shifted to more of a semi-circle. This was a reflection that the group was learning from each other, and was co-creating their own experience.

The chair arrangement in the above story is not a formula to follow, but is an example of strategic alignment of chairs.

A New Chair Arrangement for Times of Increased Complexity

More recently, I sometimes use a new chair arrangement, one that mirrors the increased complexity and uncertainty that many participants and organizations are facing these days. I scatter the chairs randomly all around the room, with no pattern, rows, or aisles. This somewhat chaotic chair arrangement seems to provide the following benefits:

1. Most participants have never been in a session with such an arrangement of chairs, so they become curious of what is about to happen, and this curiosity is a good starter for transformation.
2. The randomness of the arrangement somehow empowers the participants to move the chairs around and sit where they want. Ownership is yet another good appetizer for transformation.
3. By the end of the session, the group usually manages to rearrange the chairs into a more orderly or symmetrical setup. Hopefully, this reflects the symmetry and order that they have created together.

One other consideration is to allocate the exact number of chairs in the room as the number of participants. When all the chairs are occupied, it creates a sense of completeness within the group.

- **Play music that complements the group and the objectives**

  Music is a wonderful way to create an atmosphere of engagement. Not only is music appreciated when it complements a session, music can also become an anchor after the completion of a session.

  What genre of music is most suitable? Well, this would vary, depending on the nationality and age demographics of the participants, as well as the objectives and aspirations of the session.

  For example, playing the song "Simply the Best" at the launch of a session, shortly after the organization posted record losses and retrenched staff, would not be the right message to communicate.

  Ideally, we would play music that most, if not all the participants enjoy.

By that, I do not necessarily mean piano music, as not everyone enjoys piano music. When we ask ourselves "What music would be most suitable for this group and this session?", there is a high probability that we will come up with a good range of appropriate music. We can always ask the group "What kind of music would you like to hear?" Whoever responds, check with the rest of the group and make sure it's acceptable. Then we are ready to rock and roll, or whatever the person requested.

It helps to prepare a range of music that includes a variety of most genres or artistes. By having a wide collection of music, we have the option to cater to participants who appreciate music from their home country or generation. Besides having different genres of music and a varied list of artistes in our system, we could even create themes that are in harmony with different groups and objectives.

For example, our playlists could be categorized according to themes such as change, teamwork, inspiration, and reflection.

Here are some specific examples:

> The song "Unwritten" by Natasha Bedingfield is a meaningful song to end a session. One of the lines in the song goes: "Where your book begins, the rest is still unwritten", and this is an appropriate message for participants who are packing up and saying their goodbyes.

> For English songs, most participants seem to enjoy the music of Sting, Norah Jones and Jack Johnson, just to name a few. Apart from being engaging, many of their songs are also meaningful.

> For upbeat music that gets participants moving, there is nothing quite like bhangra music, with its origins in the Punjab region of India/Pakistan. When bhangra music is played, participants from all around the world instinctively shake their shoulders and move their hips.

> Music could also be specific to a company or an industry. If you are conducting a session for Sun Microsystems, you could create a playlist with songs about the sun or sunshine, such as "Here Comes

the Sun". And if the session is with an airline company, you can play songs about flying, such as "Come Fly with Me".

Note: Please be sure to observe the copyright laws in your country when playing music in sessions.

- **Use the wall space**
  There are a few ways to use the space on the wall as a source of learning and inspiration. One such way is to fill the walls with flipchart papers that are co-created with the group. By the end of a 2-day or 3-day session, the walls end up being decorated with all kinds of creations that are exciting and stimulating, while serving as a reminder of what has taken place.

  Besides using flipcharts, we could also use posters or banners to create visual impact. While creating an inspiring environment is helpful, it is good to remember that it could be overdone. The following story is an example of how we can balance inspiration with a touch of skepticism.

Some Cynicism in the Room May Enhance Learning

I was facilitating a 2-day session on change management and had the room filled with posters and books on change and other inspiring messages. I balanced the inspiration with a dose of cynicism, through some posters that carried skeptical messages. For example, one of the posters had a picture of a sinking ship with the word Mistakes and a note which read "It could be that the purpose of your life is to serve as a warning to others" (see www.despair.com for a full range of such posters).

At lunchtime, one of the participants told me that he was overwhelmed by all the inspirational messages when he walked into the room in the morning. He was so turned off that he almost left the session before it even started. He went on to say that he signed up for the session to learn ways to lead his department through change, not to be motivated or inspired. But just as he was about to leave the room, he caught sight of the de-motivational posters in the corner of the room and decided to stay on.

This is an example of how we can consider engaging each of the participants, even in the materials we place on the walls (refer to Strategy 3 "Go for 100%").

- **Use Visual Recording**

  Visual recording, also known as graphic recording, is a relatively new facet in facilitation, one that provides transformational impact. By using a combination of words, graphics, symbols and photos, visual recording reflects the essence of the collective wisdom and experiences of a group. A visual recorder harnesses the power of visuals that allow participants to better understand, revise, and retain the information that transpires in a session.

  A few years ago, my wife Christy started to do visual recording, and since then we have worked on many projects together.

  Apart from the stimulation that occurs within the session, visual recording provides a memorable documentation of the process. This makes it easy for participants to share their experiences and insights with those who did not attend the session.

  For example, leadership teams with visual documentation of their offsite meetings are able to communicate what they did in a powerful manner. They don't just communicate the outputs of these meetings, but they have graphics and pictures to show how the entire process unfolded to reach the outputs. The bonus is that they get to show the staff that they didn't go offsite just to play golf and sing karaoke.

  Our experience is that projects with visual recording have produced a higher level of follow-up actions, and hence, transformation. We believe this is because of the dynamic combination of the enhanced learning environment, the stimulating documentation, and the fact that they share their insights and learnings with others.

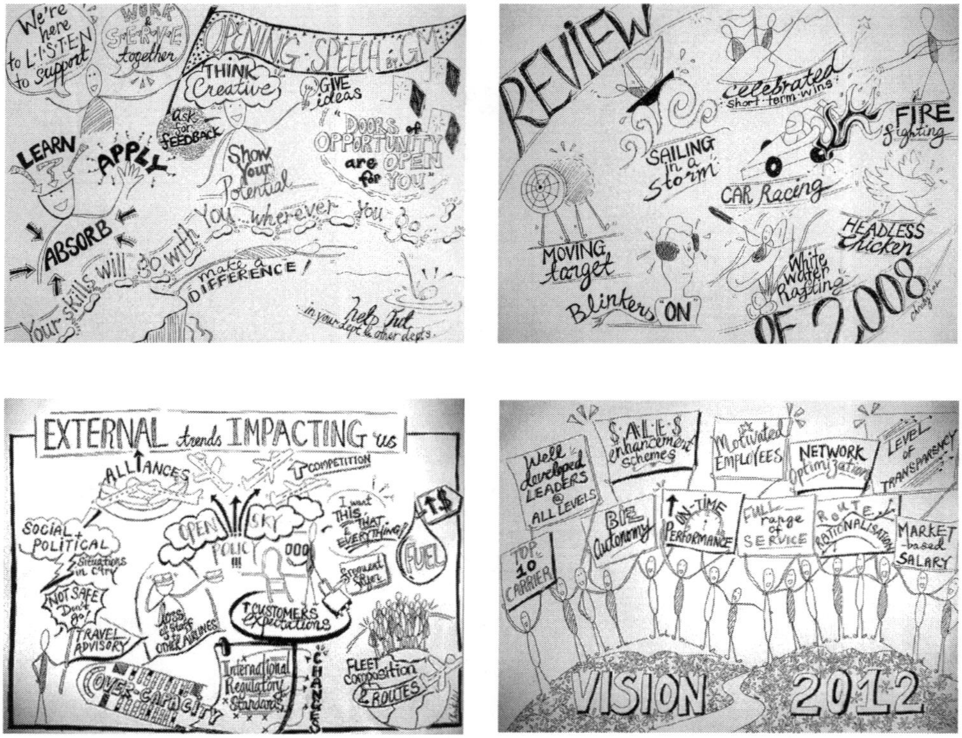

Figure 6-1: Examples of Visual Recording

For those of you who have not seen Visual Recording, the four pictures in Figure 6-1 give you an idea of what they might look like. Here you only get to see a black and white version of the original colored drawings. If you would like to learn more about visual recording, you can visit our website, www.jolc.com and look under the "What is Visual Recording" link. You can also visit the website of the International Forum of Visual Practitioners, at www.ifvp.org.

- **Display books**

  Whenever possible, bring along some books that are related to the topic of the session and display them for reading. Some participants take the time to browse through them whenever they have a few free minutes.

For residential sessions, some participants bring books back to their room for late-night reading. I usually encourage those who think they might have trouble sleeping to take the thickest book they can find, as this might help them be sound asleep after ten minutes of reading. However, there are participants who become surprisingly engaged in the book and stay up and read late into the night. Either way there is value added to the learning process. In addition to offering supplementary ideas for the topic of the session, the books often provide an extra bonus, by rekindling a passion for reading for some participants.

- **Create rituals**
  There are numerous rituals which can create a sense of rhythm and harmony in a group. One that I sometimes use is from the martial arts, where we all bow before we enter the room. I also introduce groups to "time management clapping", which is a single clap to acknowledge participant sharing. It's short, sweet, and the group claps in unison, which brings about a sense of cohesion.

  A multitude of options exist. We could request everyone to take a deep breath before we begin a session, to help us be more present to what we are going to do. We can do check-ins, asking each person to share one word or a sentence to describe how they are doing, at the beginning and end of the day. I experienced some meaningful rituals at the Authentic Leadership in Action (ALIA) Institute. Every morning starts with a short meditation, and each module begins and ends with group members bowing to each other.

- **Let the group design the room**
  This approach supersedes many of the above ideas, because this idea offers the participants the opportunity to set up their own ideal learning room. If you subscribe to the facilitator's philosophy "never work harder than the participants", this is an option to consider. Not created out of laziness,

this philosophy contains the belief that the best thing that we can do for participants is to get them more involved and engaged in the learning process.

I have used a variation of this for some multiple day sessions. On the first day, the room is fully set-up, to give participants a sense of an extensive room design. At the end of the first day, all the posters and books are removed and hidden away. When the participants show up on the morning of the second day, they are surprised to see a barren room. After having this opportunity to contrast two learning environments, they then set up the room according to what they think will maximize their learning. Besides the lesson of creating a hospitable learning environment, the participants often create amazing and stimulating designs.

- **Energize the room before participants arrive**

  My colleagues and I at AT&T had some routines to fill the room with extra energy before sessions. This is a tradition I carry on to this day, using different ways of preparing a room for the wonderful beings who are about to show up for a session. This could be as simple as taking a few deep breaths, and saying some silent intentions that every participant will create an extraordinary, transformational experience for themselves and their learning partners.

Not All Environments Are Ideal and That's OK

Sometimes we facilitate in rooms without windows, or ones that are cluttered with extra tables and chairs, or in a noisy environment. This does not mean the group is not able to create transformation. We can make the best of our situation even when the environment is not ideal, perhaps as a lesson for how to manage in a less than perfect environment.

Best wishes to you in creating transformational learning environments, whether you are in an ideal space or in the basement computer room of a dusty warehouse.

Summary

With transformation as our goal, the strategy of "Design the Environment" reminds us to treat a learning environment as a sacred site. While there is no one perfect place that is suitable for all types of sessions, there are ways of designing a space that increases the possibilities for transformation.

Some of these choices involve bright expansive views, table and chair arrangements, music, wall space, visual recording, books, rituals, group empowerment, and energizing the room.

We shape our buildings, and afterwards our buildings shape us.
– Winston Churchill

Reflection Questions

1. How purposeful are you in designing and creating learning environments?
2. Do you attempt to align your room set-up with the theme and objectives of the session?
3. Do participants in the sessions you facilitate gain extra inspiration from elements of the learning environment?

Insights and Expansions

What did you find most interesting about this strategy?

____

____

How can you build your capacity to Design The Environment?

____

____

Where to go from here?

If you are reading in sequence, the next strategy has to do with the language of transformation. If you haven't read Strategy 5 "Design for Transformation" yet, there are ideas there on overall design.

In the spirit of design, you can write out the numbers 1-12 with your less dominant writing hand, and find the number that has the most interesting design. This work of art becomes your next strategy to read. *enJOY!*

Strategy 7

MIND YOUR LANGUAGE

Language exerts hidden power, like the moon on the tides.
– Rita Mae Brown

Always and never are two words you should always remember never to use.
– Wendell Johnson

We cannot guarantee transformation, but we can create an environment that increases the possibility of breakthrough shifts. Part of the environment is created by the way we express ourselves as facilitators. In this strategy we will explore the power of language. We will do this with an introduction of a language acronym called CLEAR, followed by a table of distinctions between typical and CLEAR phrases.

Being mindful about our language becomes particularly important at the end of a session. We will explore ways of communicating with participants that supports them in implementing whatever shifts and plans they create in the session.

It's Language and It's More Than Just Language

In this strategy, we examine the power of the words we use. There is more to what we communicate than just through words; there are our non-verbals (tone of voice, body language, etc.), our intentions, and the level of congruency between what we say and who we are (some people will know if we are incongruent). So while our words convey a message to others, there is more to these messages than just saying a few well-chosen phrases. In this section however, we will focus on language, and you can imagine ways of being that would be congruent with the way we speak.

When we are immersed in the spirit of breakthrough and our intentions are clear, our message is normally aligned. However, there could be occasions when we are less effective in facilitating transformation due to our choice of words, and this is the purpose of this section.

Using CLEAR Language

If you wish to know the mind of a man, listen to his words.
– Chinese Proverb

When we facilitate, we are presented with many opportunities to choose words and phrases that increase an individual and group's sense of ownership and learning.

Thus, how do we make our language CLEAR, in order to enhance the chances of transformation occurring in a session? Well, here is an acronym that offers some guidelines for us to remember:

Clarity–to lessen the chances of confusion or resistance
Leverage wisdom–the participants in the room are the experts
Expand possibilities–invite exploration from each and all
Avoid generalizations–show discerning thought
Reality–check assumptions, and provide engagement

To illustrate CLEAR language, the examples in Figure 7-1 make distinctions between somewhat typical language used in sessions, in contrast to what more

CLEAR language sounds like. As you go through the table below, reflect on what you usually say, and consider if there is a way to alter your choice of words, to be more transformational. If you are in the mood for some instant transformation, you can improve on the language in the "CLEAR Language" column.

TYPICAL LANGUAGE	CLEAR LANGUAGE
"This session will change your life."	"Many people have attended this session and made significant changes in their lives. Our hope is that you will discover ideas and tools that can support you in resolving your most pressing issues and in creating more of the life you aspire to create."
"You are going to have lots of fun here." (This sets up all kinds of expectations which we may not want, may not be able to fulfill, or that others may not find relevant.)	"We trust you will find ways to learn a lot here, and we also hope that you enjoy the learning process."
"We will be asking you for feedback at the end of the session."	"At the end of the session, we will be asking for your feedback. We will also ask you to reflect on how you feel about your level of participation and engagement."
"You need to give 110% of yourself in order to get the most from this session." (Is it possible to give 110%?)	"You have probably attended many sessions before, so what can you do to maximize your learning while you are here?"
"I know that some of you may not want to be here, but now that you are here, you might as well make the best of it."	"As you introduce yourself, please also share how you feel about being here."
"These processes and tools really work."	"Be skeptical and open, and see how these ideas can help you back at work."

Figure 7-1: Typical Language vs CLEAR Language *(continued)*

"You must get out of your comfort zone if you want to learn anything here."	"Most people say they learn the most when they were out of their comfort zone. If that's true for you, then notice when you are feeling slightly on the edge of your comfort zone, and know that you are entering the learning zone. Of course, don't go too far out and end up in the twilight zone."
"How can you fix that problem?"	"If that problem was resolved, what would you be seeing?" or "What similar challenges have you successfully managed?"
"Please talk fast. We are running short on time."	"We have 30 minutes for this sharing session. How can we best manage the time, and would someone be willing to be our timekeeper?"
"That is a good answer, exactly what I was looking for."	"How does that sound to everyone else?" or "That is a good answer, because..."
"That is a great question." (This could be ok to say, however, it can sound phony or patronizing, especially if it is overused)	"Let's explore that. What do you all think?" or "That question shows you are making useful distinctions between...", or just answer the question.
"You don't find this to be practical? Are you sure you gave it a fair chance?"	"Please tell us why you don't think this tool is practical for you." or "Who else is wondering about the practical applications of this tool?"
"We need to... " or "We have to... " or "We should... " (which implies there is no choice)	"We are going to... so it will enable us to..."
"I will now split you into groups." or "I want you to sit with people you don't know."	"Let's split into groups." or "Can you arrange yourselves in small groups with people you don't know very well?"

Figure 7-1: Typical Language vs CLEAR Language *(continued)*

"This section is quite difficult, so do your best to stay awake."	"This next section of the session has been known to be quite stimulating and challenging, and thus provides us with many opportunities for breakthroughs." (or redesign the section of the session if it is not interesting enough)
"Are you clear?" or "Do you have any questions?"	"What questions or ideas do you have to help make this clearer?"
"I don't understand why you don't get this point."	"Sorry if I wasn't clear. Let me try again." or "Can someone help us out and explain this point more clearly?"
"Other groups did this much better than you did."	"There are other ways of doing this which can be more effective. What ideas do you have on what you could have done differently?"
"People don't listen to each other anymore."	"You may have noticed that sometimes you don't listen as deeply as you would like. What can you do to help remind yourself to listen to others in ways that will deepen your understanding and your relationships?"
"I can see that everyone is tired." (or confused, bored, hopeful, etc.)	"How many of you are feeling tired?" (or confused, bored, hopeful, etc.)
"It's human nature", "Men/women are... " (or any other generalization)	Be mindful of any generalizations. If used, be sure to be clear it is a generalization.
"Let's talk about the way you manage your subordinates." ("subordinates" translates to sub-ordinary)	"Let's explore how to more effectively lead the people who report to you."

Figure 7-1: Typical Language vs CLEAR Language *(continued)*

"Now the hard work begins, going back to the real world."	"We are now going to complete the session. What are some of the obstacles you are going to face and how can you sustain the momentum and learning from here?" (more on this later in the strategy)

Figure 7-1: Typical Language vs CLEAR Language *(continued)*

What are your reflections after going through the list in Figure 7-1? Between the two columns, in which one do you spend more time? What additions and refinements would you make to the list?

As we are not always able to prepare the right choice of words for every situation, we can "Be Intentional" (Strategy 1) and "Be Present with Presence" (Strategy 2). When we are intentional, present, and mindful of our language, there is an excellent chance that the seeds of transformation are being planted.

Mind Your Language, at the Completion of a Session

Even the best of sessions fail to deliver their full potential if participants do not apply their learning after they leave the session. To encourage participants, many well-intentioned facilitators communicate something like the following:

"This session would have been a waste of your time unless you go back and apply your learning. So best wishes to you as you return to the real world, where the hard work begins."

Have you ever heard something like this before? What are your thoughts about this message? Here are some of my reflections on that statement:

1. Hopefully no session would ever be a total waste of time, as there are bound to be insights, connections, and reminders that serve a participant's journey in life, whether they apply their learning directly, or indirectly.

2. How do most participants react to the idea of returning to more hard work? This message seems to decrease the chances of a participant applying their learning.
3. What is the real world? It seems to me that participants are usually more real and authentic in learning sessions. Whenever I ask participants whether they feel more real in the environment of the session or in their everyday work life, they say that they are more real in the session. So instead of bringing our learning back to the real world, perhaps we can bring more realness and authenticity back to our organizations and communities.

What Is a More Effective Way to Complete a Session?

By using words that are authentic and encouraging, the following phrase serves as an alternative way to complete a session:

"Many of you have made commitments to do things differently after attending this session. But about a month from now, it is highly possible that you will not have implemented everything you said you would. At that point, you will have two choices: one is to invalidate the time spent here, and the other is to re-commit yourself to your action plans.

Understand that not applying all of your learning is normal, and that this session has been a real experience. Forgetting is quite normal, but in the act of remembering, you can re-commit yourself to whatever you think is important. As Jean Houston said, '...by forgetting, we gain the joy of remembering'."

How does this closing sound to you?

Supporting Follow-Through Action

There are many factors which influence whether a participant will put what they have learned into use, such as the culture of the organization, support from the boss, etc. Also, there seems to be a common belief that the impact of learning sessions do not last. With so many challenges facing the transfer of learning, let's be sure to equip participants with some tools for enhanced resilience as they leave the session.

We can offer and brainstorm options on what participants can say to themselves when they successfully implement one of the ideas or plans from the session. They can celebrate and say: "Wow, I am getting better at following through," or "I know how to put my learning into action."

On the other hand, we can explore what can be done when participants do not fully implement their action plans. They can simply ask: "What do I still want to do?" or, "What tools could be useful for me right now?"

By bringing such possibilities into the forefront, participants can effectively process the successes and setbacks they will face in their implementation plans. This way of processing events is relevant in all aspects of life (for more on this, you can read *Learned Optimism* and the *The Optimistic Child* by Martin Seligman).

Summary

When we honor the spirit of transformation and do our best to be mindful of our language, amazing things can happen. I have noticed that as my language becomes clearer and more transformational over the years, less time is spent trying to clarify points, and more time is dedicated to exploring meaningful issues.

I hope that this strategy has provided some reminders for you. Let us allow ourselves to be guided to use the language that serves the highest good and highest possibility for transformation.

You probably found some faults in my language in this section, or in the other parts of the book. If so, an email to dougo@jolc.com would be much appreciated. Thanks in advance for your feedback.

Our language is funny–a fat chance and
a slim chance mean the same thing.
– J. Gustav White

Reflection Questions

1. How mindful are you in using CLEAR language during a session, and in your life?
2. Are you able to conclude sessions in a manner that provides the participants with effective ways to manage their return to their work and life?

Insights and Expansions

What did you find most interesting about this strategy?

____

____

How can you build your capacity to Mind Your Language?

____

____

Where to go from here?

If you work with teams, you might want to move ahead to Strategy 8 "Breakthrough with Teams". If not, you might want to move on to Strategy 9 "Be a Transformer." If you do not feel like making a choice right now, you can look around and find the first number you see from 1 to 12. That number could be the next strategy to read... trust it will be perfect.

Strategy 8

BREAKTHROUGH WITH TEAMS

Never doubt that a small group of thoughtful, committed, citizens can change the world. Indeed, it is the only thing that ever has.
– Margaret Mead

If you want to build a ship, don't drum up people together to collect wood and don't assign them tasks and work, but rather teach them to long for the endless immensity of the sea.
– Antoine de Saint-Exupery

Working with teams offers unique opportunities for transformation. Many of these opportunities occur before the session begins, in the planning phase. There are also a number of processes that can plant the seeds of transformation once the session has begun.

In this strategy, we will use the word "team" to represent any group of people who work together for a common goal or passion, with interdependencies in what they do, e.g. members of a team, department, leadership team, community, or organization.

Our Role as Permission Givers

From the first meeting with a client, until the completion of an intervention, team sessions offer an opportunity to explore issues that people do not seem to be able to bring up in the normal course of working life. Often these are issues which are critical to the team and organization success. Sometimes I think of my role as a "Permission Giver", giving team members the chance to discuss their key issues with the larger system.

In this chapter, we will explore ideas on how to capitalize on these opportunities and offer permission to team members to discuss what is important to them.

Potential Derailers of Team Transformation

During the planning for a session, we are able to examine issues which are more or less likely to create breakthroughs for a team. As we go through the process of identifying the relevant issues for the team, there are signs to look out for, ones that could give us a warning that transformation will be more difficult to achieve.

Here are a few derailers to keep an ear out for:

- "FIX MY TEAM!" Leaders often want a session because team members do not take enough initiative, or are not creative, or do not work well together. These are all reasonable requests. However, senior leaders usually play an important role in team dynamics. During the planning process, it is helpful, but not always easy, to ask the senior leader(s): "Are you willing to look at your role in the current situation, and consider the possibility that you might need to change, in order to create shifts in the team?" Their answer to this question says a lot. Peter Block's two books on "Flawless Consulting" are great resources to learn more about the contracting phase of an engagement.
- "THIS PROGRAM WILL FIX US." A good session helps teams along the way, but it is just part of a process, not the end point. Team members are well-served to remember that. While our goal is transformation, it is difficult to make promises, because we are not the ones who do the transforming.

- "IT WILL WORK IF WE DO A FOLLOW-UP." Follow-up is important, but it is not "the answer". What about a follow-up to the follow-up? At some point, team leaders and members can choose to take accountability for their own success and their own development process. Their ownership might include becoming process consultants to their own work, creating a culture of openness and support, and looking at processes and structures that can build team capacity and ensure effectiveness and sustainability.

These potential derailers can help us determine whether doing a session is the optimal path to follow. It is possible that the most transformational way forward is not to do a session, and the strategies of this book can help guide us in the planning process as well. Being present with the client and aligning intentions are a good foundation for anything that follows, including a decision not to plan a workshop.

Other possibilities for an intervention include executive coaching or a dialogue on the systemic factors that might be causing the stated challenges. There is also the possibility of delaying a session until the timing is more suitable, or finding an elegant way to withdraw from the project in a way that still serves the client.

Let's assume we managed to identify and avoid some of the potential derailers of working with teams. We can now turn our attention to ideas for increasing transformational opportunities in the planning process.

Get Participants Involved Before the Session

Give team members the opportunity to take ownership of whatever is about to emerge, early on in the planning stage. The following are four methodologies, each offering possibilities for transformation to occur even before the official session commences.

Ways of Engaging a Team Before a Session–Jumpstarting Transformation

1. Surveys: Real-Time Administration and Processing

My favorite way of engaging with a team is to meet with them as part of the pre-session planning process. This is an opportunity to administer a survey of what is happening in the team, and to find out what they would like from a workshop. One question on the survey is whether an offsite meeting is a good idea to begin with. The surveys are administered and the data is quickly processed to produce a team report. When the team receives the report, the data is literally and figuratively "hot off the presses". Then small groups analyze the data and report to the entire group.

Here are two examples of how these surveys helped to create breakthroughs:

- A General Manager (GM) and Human Resource (HR) Director were excited to be organizing an offsite planning meeting for their leadership team. After the survey was completed, the team found that their score in favor of an offsite was about a "3" out of "7". The GM and the team then engaged in an enriching dialogue on different ways to do their planning process. So the transformation in this case was not doing a workshop, and the team being more purposeful about how they do their planning.
- According to the results of a particular survey, the priority for a department retreat was to develop work plans and to re-look at their vision, mission, and values. Normally these types of objectives can be challenging for a group of 80 participants, and even the Department Head was surprised that the department members were so enthusiastic about the survey data. But because the group had chosen these objectives, they did some extraordinary work together at the retreat.

Note: The process described in point 1 is ideally done a month or two in advance of a planned retreat. This can also be done at the session itself, because the data will be fresh. However, the main advantages of doing it as part of the pre-session planning are that the group decides whether it is a good idea to even have a retreat, they can offer valuable input into the design, while also taking ownership of the process.

2. **Conference Calls**

   Most geographically dispersed teams have regular conference calls. So as a facilitator of an event, we can join in a call to begin the engagement process. Once I was working with a global team, where I was warned in advance that the leaders were too busy to do any pre-work. In this case, the preliminary design of the session had three significant pieces of pre-work. So when I joined one of their scheduled conference calls to solicit their feedback, I was surprised that not only did the leaders offer a number of good ideas, but even agreed to complete the pre-work in a timely manner, which they did.

3. **Phone or In-person Interviews**

   One-on-one interviews are an excellent way to build rapport, get to know the participants better, and get a clearer picture of what is happening in the organization. An option which has proven to be effective is to talk/meet each of the individuals before AND after the session, with the post-session meeting being a coaching session. This is an example of a transformational process.

4. **Emails and/or Online Survey**

   Sometimes it is not possible to connect with the participants in any of the above ways, but even an email can plant the seeds for transformation. In this case, a welcome note with an introduction, some objectives and a tentative outline is a good start, and perhaps an online survey. One important element of the pre-session email is to encourage participants to provide their feedback on what needs to happen in order for them to consider the session to be an effective investment of their time and energy. I also ask them to share what they think would get in the way of a successful session, and what they do NOT want to see at the workshop."

From this above section, you can see that there are many ways to get participants involved and engaged in the planning process.

We will now shift our attention from the planning stage to the actual session. What can we do to be more purposeful in planting the seeds for breakthrough with teams, once a session has begun? Here are eight ideas:

1. Ask the group if they are ready for transformation

We can ask the group if they want to make transformation their goal. If they answer "YES", we can ask them what it might look like and how they think it can be accomplished. If they hesitate or say "NO", we can engage in a dialogue with them. It could be that they think there are barriers that are stopping them from making significant shifts, or maybe they feel they have already done enough transforming and now it's time for consolidation.

2. Allow each participant to share in the beginning of a session

An effective way to plant seeds of transformation is to give each member a chance to share with the entire group, early in the session and in a powerful manner. Often participants are asked, "What are your expectations of this session?", but this question places the responsibility for success on the whole group, or on the facilitator, which is not powerful or effective.

A more effective set of questions for participants to answer in front of their team is:

a. "What would you like to say to your teammates as you begin the next stage of your journey together?"

b. "What are your intentions for what you can co-create together in this session?"

c. "What will you do to ensure that this session is successful?"

By the time each person has shared, amazing breakthroughs may have already occurred. In a large group, where it could be difficult to hear from everyone, sharing can be done in small groups and then summarized for the large group.

3. Give the team a chance to share their feelings

When I share this idea with a client, sometimes I am told that "our leaders don't like to talk about their feelings". Fair enough. So instead of asking them "How do you feel?" we can rephrase the question.

The "Future Search" process, described briefly in Strategy 5 "Design For Transformation", includes a section for groups to express their "Prouds and Sorries" for the work that they have done together. You don't have to be facilitating a "Future Search" to use this part of the process. An alternative for the wording can be "Glads, Sads, and Mads", but the idea is the same. Sometimes the act of sharing emotions, rather than just talking about numerical targets, can create the significant energy for change.

4. Be sure the team has numerous opportunities to make relevant connections back to their work

Even the most practical theories and frameworks need to be applied to the participant's everyday life. What better way to build a team than to work on the issues and challenges that contribute to the team's success? Team members look forward to the opportunity to openly discuss the issues that most impact their work.

5. Introduce practical models and frameworks

Kurt Lewin said, "There is nothing as practical as a good theory." Practical theories provide teams a common language to refer to, even after the session has completed.

There are many team models to choose from. You probably have some favorites, and here are a few I have found to be useful:

- The "Form-Storm-Norm-Perform" model developed by Bruce Tuckman. Teams can use this framework to evaluate themselves, and are reminded that healthy storming (disagreement, not arguments) is a key to success.
- The "GRIP" model developed by Richard Beckhard (he called it "GRPI") is a helpful framework. The "GRIP" acronym stands for: Goals, Roles, Interpersonal Norms, and Processes. Apart from being a diagnostic tool, this framework can help teams get a GRIP on their success. An internet search will yield lists of questions that could be used for assessment and dialogue in the four areas.
- "The 3-Legged Stool" from the *Fifth Discipline Fieldbook* is an apt metaphor for organization success, and the accompanying frameworks and tools contain lots of depth and breadth. The three legs of the stool represent the core learning capabilities: Personal/Shared Aspirations, Generative Conversation/Collaboration, and Conceptualization/Seeing Systems.
- I sometimes give a copy of *Five Dysfunctions of a Team* or the *Four Obsessions of an Extraordinary Executive* by Patrick Lencioni, to a senior leader in an initial meeting. If the leader finds the book relevant, it is assigned as pre-reading for all participants. Reading these leadership fables can be transformational for leaders, and the pre-reading creates a framework and language for the session.

Models like those described above can help create an ongoing common language for teams. One of the many benefits of doing preplanning work with a team is to get a good idea of which model(s) would be the best match to help them achieve their vision and goals.

6. Give everyone a chance to talk

A session provides an opportunity to hear from each person on a range of issues. Often in teams it is the loudest, most extroverted, or higher-level persons who determine the direction and influence decision-making.

We can create discussion structures (i.e., "go-arounds" or "check-ins/check-outs") in which every team member can share their thoughts, feelings, and ideas on what is happening in the organization, or what they would like to see.

A simple engagement technique is a "passion check", where an idea is evaluated on a scale of 1–10 and everyone gives their rating; this allows for maximum involvement in a short time, and the group gets an instant assessment of the idea.

Giving everyone an opportunity to share their ideas is not just a nice thing to do. There are at least three significant potential benefits from hearing from everyone:

a. Momentum is generated, as once individuals begin sharing, it gets easier after that, especially for those who are usually less expressive.
b. Trust is built, as team members share and listen in a non-judgmental manner.
c. A more comprehensive collective picture emerges from the group.

7. Tune in to the team dynamics

Usually, how a team acts in a session has parallels to how they act in their work life. Being able to help a team identify those dynamics can assist them in transforming the way they work.

One such intervention happened years ago when I was at AT&T, for a 5-day team session that I was attending. On the morning of the third day, the facilitator shared a perception with us, that she felt we were not a high-performing team. We were shocked to hear this and asked her where she drew this conclusion from. She pointed out that a couple of team members had not spoken much in the first two days. In her opinion, no team could be considered high-performing without tapping into the experiences and wisdom of all of its members.

This was a wake-up call for us. As we processed the implications of this observation, we committed ourselves to hear from everyone on the team on a regular basis, even if all a person said was that they agreed with what was happening.

8. Agree on what to communicate to those who were not at the team session

Setting aside time to get clarity on messages to communicate to others is beneficial for participants at the session, as well as for those who were not present. The participants consolidate important decisions and ideas, and then create a message that is consistent and aligned. Those who were not at the session get to hear not only one person's perspective, but a collective view of what transpired.

Summary

A session with a team can be rewarding and transformational, and can create powerful and inspiring short and long-term results. Pre-session planning fertilizes the soil to plant the seeds of transformation, and engages team members in meaningful interactions which enables those seeds to sprout into full blooms. Best wishes to all of us as we facilitate this meaningful work.

When spider webs unite, they can tie up a lion.
– An African Proverb

Reflection Questions

1. How are you at engaging clients before any intervention, in a way that plants the seeds of transformation?
2. How are you at creating a safe environment and giving participants the "permission" to share their perspectives?
3. How many models of team effectiveness are you aware of, as well as practical theories to use with teams?

Insights and Expansions

What did you find most interesting about this strategy?

____

____

How can you build your capacity to Breakthrough With Teams?

____

____

Where to go from here?

You can proceed with the book sequentially and move on to Strategy 9 "Be a Transformer", or you can let your intuition guide you to the next strategy. If you choose to let your intuition guide you, turn to the table of contents and allow a strategy to choose you. Either way, honor your choice and enJOY the process.

Strategy 9

BE A TRANSFORMER

In my early professional years I was asking the question:
How can I treat, or cure, or change this person?
Now I would phrase the question in this way:
How can I provide a relationship which this person may
use for his/her own personal growth?
– Carl Rogers

Perhaps we can start thinking of ourselves not as human beings,
but as human becomings.
– Rob Brezsny

In this strategy, we will explore renowned psychologist Dr. Carl Roger's "person-centered approach" to psychotherapy, and add in the importance of asking good questions.

Dr. Rogers wrote that the three conditions of a person-centered approach are genuineness, unconditional positive regard, and empathic understanding. According to him, "There is a body of steadily mounting research evidence, which by and large supports the view that when these facilitative conditions are present, changes in personality and behavior do indeed occur." (*Way of Being*, pg 117)

Even though Dr. Rogers wrote this regarding a client-therapist relationship, these three conditions and the ability to ask powerful questions have parallels to our work as facilitators. In this strategy, we will look at how these four ingredients relate to our work, and how we can expand our capacity to be genuine, to give unconditional positive regard to others, to be an empathic listener, and to ask powerful questions.

We will begin our exploration with the first of these conditions, being genuine.

Genuineness

When we are authentic, we build trust and give others permission to be authentic as well.

> *Learn to be quiet enough to hear the genuine within yourself so that you can hear it in others.*
> – Marian Wright Edelman

Whether it is sharing a story about a personal challenge in applying some of the tools, or simply being open with the group about how we are feeling in the moment, we are displaying genuineness.

What follows is a story about making a choice on whether or not to speak my thoughts with a group.

A Moment of Truth

I was facilitating a departmental retreat, which began after dinner on a Friday evening. The director opened the gathering by telling everyone that she was going to give a short opening speech, and on Sunday afternoon would share her more substantial reflections. Her short welcome speech was a 30–40 minute monologue and group members were beginning to doze off.

When I was introduced to the group, I had an internal dilemma, which felt like a moment of truth. Do I just begin the session as planned, or do I acknowledge the fact that this short speech was not so short?

Considering that one of the objectives of the weekend session was for the team members to be more open with one another, I decided to walk the talk. So after the director introduced me, I asked her, "If that was the short speech, then how much time should be allocated for the longer summary on Sunday?"

After a brief instant, the director laughed, and then everyone burst into laughter. Being a good sport, she did a quick recovery, apologized to the group for getting carried away, and said that her talk on Sunday would be shorter, so that everyone could go home to their families. We went on to have a marvelous and memorable session, with lots of openness and breakthroughs.

Was this approach risky? It felt like it was. Was I nervous when I was about to ask her the question? Yes! But my inner voice was telling me that sharing openly was the right thing to do. If I had just gone along with the program without commenting about the long speech, the breakthroughs in the session might have been less significant.

In this situation, my intention was not to embarrass the director. On the contrary, I trusted that she was able to handle the question professionally and with elegance, which she did. I also believed that the approach was for the highest good for the session and the organization.

Being 100% open and sharing all our thoughts is neither prudent nor effective. But it does challenge us to think about how open we can be, and in a way that sets the stage for breakthroughs. While I chose to speak up in the above story and it worked out well, there were a number of times in similar situations that I chose not to say anything. Here are the criteria I use when deciding whether or not to share openly in front of a group:

1. Is my intuition telling me it's the right thing to do?
2. Am I clear that this will serve the highest good of the person and the group?

If the answer to both questions is "Yes", I take a deep breath and speak up. Otherwise, I wait to see what emerges as the session unfolds.

The following story is about a new facilitator who had a choice to make about how authentic to be in his self introduction at the start of a workshop.

To Be or Not to Be Authentic, That Was the Question

Soft-spoken and new to working with groups, a facilitator was preparing his brief introduction for the next morning. He was unsure if it was best to acknowledge the fact that he had never facilitated before. Caught in a dilemma, he began to weigh the advantages and disadvantages of being authentic about his lack of experience. He asked for advice, but the rest of the team, including myself, told him that either way would be alright.

After a night's sleep, or perhaps a night of tossing and turning, here is how he introduced himself to the group: "Hi everyone, my name is Chee Hian and I am from the IT Department. I have never facilitated a session before, so I apologize in advance for the mistakes that I will make over the next two days. At this point, you might be wondering why I am here. Well, I am here because I am passionate about continuing the miracle spirit we have created in our company. I am so passionate that I am willing to spend lots of time preparing for this, with the opportunity to serve you on this journey we are on together."

This display of genuineness created an instant shift in the room, and the session went on to be an extraordinary experience for everyone who was there.

As you can see from the above story, being genuine and authentic is a good place to start on the journey of being a transformer. We will now look into Dr. Roger's next ingredient for being a transformer, which is unconditional positive regard.

Unconditional Positive Regard

From my observation, most teachers and facilitators claim to love people. This was also true for me when I began my work as a facilitator. However, there is one catch to this, and it is a big one: there seems to be a lot of people who seem difficult to love. Are you able to relate to this at all?

> *Treat people as if they were who they ought to be, and you help them become who they are capable of being.*
> – Johann von Goethe

This came as a shock to me, as I believed I loved people. Yet, I found myself struggling to like quite a number of participants in some sessions. This bothered me a lot, and I re-examined this love of people belief I thought I had.

It was then I started to adopt a new credo, which was to learn to love and appreciate even the most difficult people. After all these years, this journey still feels like a "2 steps forward, 1 step back" trip, but at least I am moving ahead on the path.

A wonderful lesson in this area is that the people whom we allow ourselves to be irritated by are often our best teachers. After all, how we feel about others is often more of a reflection of ourselves, rather than the other party. For instance, have you ever made a comment about someone after a meeting or a session, that a person "was so loud", and a friend counters "but I liked the extra energy he brought to the group"? And even if your friend agreed with you, the challenge remains how to honor the person and learn how to interact with him in the most effective manner, and to learn from the situation.

Can you think of a participant type that you find challenging to appreciate? For me, the participants who are most difficult to accept and love are those who nitpick or challenge more than seems appropriate to me.

We are presented with learning opportunities every time we meet someone we do not like or fully accept. They expand our capacity to give unconditional positive regard, which is an example of how much we learn when we work with groups. As Carl Jung said, "Everything that irritates us about others can lead us to an understanding of ourselves."

The following story sheds some light on how personal reflection led to some transformation for me, and for some others.

Reflecting on Self and Appreciating Others

I was facilitating a month-long module on the topic of facilitation. One of the participants challenged and questioned a lot of things we did in the course. Even though I thanked him for his perspectives and/or asked the group for their thoughts each time he spoke up, I felt frustrated with all of the challenges and the time taken to answer his queries.

I wanted to be genuine and share my thoughts with him, but I did not know how to do this in an effective manner (as you can see, I am still working on being more genuine). I asked myself: "What do I appreciate about him, and why am I bothered by him?" I realized that his courage to speak up in front of the group was a gift that he brought to the course (especially in East Asian culture, where people are often reserved about sharing in front of a big group). I also saw that some of my irritation with him was due to my own reticence to challenge facilitators in sessions that I attended.

With this insight, I then shared my reflections with the group at the next session. I thanked him for his courage to speak up and acknowledged his willingness to deepen everyone's understanding of the topics. I also expressed my concern that the discussions were taking time from other worthwhile topics in the session.

This then led to an open dialogue on how we could strike a balance of dealing with questions and managing our time together. Through this dialogue, some shifts occurred for that participant and for me, while the rest of the group had the experience of such open reflection.

When we can transform our perspectives about others, magical things can happen. When we explore our own blockages and frustrations, we expand our capacity to give unconditional positive regard in the future.

So when you find yourself frustrated with a participant the next time, you can ask yourself these questions:

1. Why do you allow yourself to get frustrated with this participant?
2. What do you appreciate about this person?
3. What can you say or do that would be authentic and show unconditional positive regard for this participant?

Having looked at the first two ingredients for becoming a transformer, we will now proceed to the third, empathic understanding.

Empathic Understanding

We have just explored how a learning environment is enhanced when people feel accepted. Another element for enhanced learning is ensuring that people feel listened to and understood. When we empathize with participants, we create a shared reality and connection. The resulting rapport can plant seeds for tremendous growth and development.

This area of empathic understanding is a challenge for me. When someone shares a problem or concern, my tendency is to give advice, or tell them not to worry. Despite the good intentions, neither of these approaches facilitates much support.

One of the easiest human acts is also one of the most healing. Listening to someone. Simply listening. Not advising or coaching, but silently and fully listening.
– Margaret Wheatley

When people have a problem or an issue at hand, they would have already thought of some possible solutions, and most of the time would like a listening ear, not a problem-solver. From my experience, few people are skillful in empathic listening, which is both good and bad news. The bad news is that most people do not feel listened to very often (is that true for you?). The good news is that every act of empathic listening can make a difference in the lives of others, because it is a rare experience for many people.

By reflecting on someone's feelings before we discuss the situation, we display some understanding of what the person is going through, or at least show that we are trying. As facilitators, our ability to create rapport with participants is a key element in the effectiveness of our work. After the feelings are addressed and the connection is made, we can dialogue on the issues they have raised.

In the following section, we will employ a different learning methodology; you have the opportunity to practice and assess your empathic understanding with two different exercises.

Empathic Understanding–Exercise 1

Instructions: Read the statement from the participant. Then refer to the four possible responses from a facilitator and choose the one that you think would be a typical response and the one that would be the most empathic response.

1. Participant: "I want to attend this session, but I've got a million things to do back at the office."

   Possible responses from facilitator:

   A. Well, just make the most of the time here and catch up with your work in the evenings.

   B. Do you think you're important just because you're busy?

   C. You sound overwhelmed. Is there a way that I can support your being here?

   D. Only a million? Last week, there was a person here with two million things to do.

   Typical ____________________ Empathic ____________________

2. Participant: "The only reason I'm here is because my boss forced me to come."

   Possible responses from facilitator:

   A. Now that you're here, how do you feel?

   B. Your boss must be a difficult person to work for.

   C. Now that you are here, you might as well make the best of it.

   D. If your boss told you to take a leap off the Great Wall of China, would you?

   Typical ____________________ Empathic ____________________

3. Participant: "This is the best session I've ever been to. My life has changed because of the past three days."

   Possible responses from facilitator:

   A. Don't get too excited, this is only a temporary high.
   B. Wow! You sound excited about what has happened here... happy to hear that. Tell me how you feel your life has changed.
   C. That's great. Well, it's all because you engaged in the process and are such a good learner.
   D. I felt that way too after I attended this session.

   Typical ____________________ Empathic ____________________

4. Participant: "All this talk about planning and problem-solving is great, but we don't have time in the real world to plan, or to do proper problem-solving."

   Possible responses from facilitator:

   A. Well, whose fault is that?
   B. We offer a course in time management, I'll get you a brochure.
   C. Don't worry. After this course, you'll now have more tools to plan and solve problems in shorter timeframes.
   D. You must be frustrated when things don't get planned properly.

   Typical ____________________ Empathic ____________________

Here are some thoughts on the four scenarios. These are not necessarily the correct answers, but just my opinion, worth about two cents in your local currency.

Number 1:

My experience is that "A" is a well-intentioned and typical response, but the participant would not feel heard. A "C" response lets the participant know that we empathize with them, and we can then explore ways to handle the situation.

Number 2:

The essence of this scenario is similar to number 1, with "C" being a typical response and "A" being the one that offers a good connection between the participant and us.

Number 3:

Here, we get to practice empathy with an enthusiastic participant, rather than a troubled one. I plead guilty to having used "C" too many times. Do you agree that "C" would be the most typical response? As for the most empathic response, my vote goes to "B" because lots of insights are likely to arise from that question, for both the participant and the facilitator.

Number 4:

Well, choosing the typical response for number 4 is challenging. Depending on the facilitator, both "B" and "C" responses seem possible, but we could almost predict how a participant would feel after hearing either of those statements. "D" is not a magical response, but at least it lets the participants know they have been heard.

Please note that these empathic responses do not signal the end of the conversation. On the contrary, they are meant to foster a stronger connection with the participant, and to catapult the dialogue to higher levels. Later in the conversation we may even use some of the typical responses from above, but not as the initial response.

How are you feeling about your empathic understanding abilities? To facilitate more practice, we are going to use a different format in Exercise 2.

Empathic Understanding–Exercise 2

Instructions: Imagine that the following statements were expressed by a participant during a one-on-one conversation with you. Fill in the blanks with what you think would be a good, empathic response.

1. Participant: "That last activity was a total waste of time."

   You respond with:

   ____

2. Participant: "All this talk about teamwork and communication is nonsense. Once they get back to the office, everybody will go back to their old, selfish ways, playing politics."

   You respond with:

   ____

3. Participant: "I would prefer not to be here today. My family is spending the day at the beach and I would really like to be with them."

   You respond with:

   ____

4. Participant: "Thanks to you and this session, our team is finally back on track. I feel that we'll be able to maintain this trust and open communication and be more successful."

   You respond with:

   ____

How empathic are your responses? What follows are once again not the standard answers, but just some thoughts on what might be effective responses.

Number 1:

"You seem frustrated with that activity. Thanks for being willing to share your thoughts, I appreciate that. As for the activity, please tell me what makes you say it was a waste of time." Most likely the person will feel heard, and then will share their thoughts on the activity. We can learn a lot from someone who is willing to speak their mind in a situation like this.

Number 2:

"You have a perception that people don't change in your team?" This would provide the participant with the chance to reflect and share more. After which, you could always follow up with more challenging questions like "Have you changed from sessions like this?", "How do you deal with office politics?", or "What can you do to shift the way things are done?"

Number 3:

"It sounds like your family is important to you and you miss spending time with them." It is tempting to think that the participant is complaining about being at the session. While this might be true to some extent, what they are saying is that they miss their family.

Number 4:

"You sound happy about the result. That's fantastic. How can you ensure that the effects stay long-lasting?"

Notice that the above responses allow the participants to reflect and share more of their thoughts, which in turn, increases the chances for good rapport and high-quality dialogue.

With regards to the above items, I have a hunch that some of you may have better suggested answers. If so, please email them to me at dougo@jolc.com for a future edition of this book.

One more area to explore in this "Be a Transformer" strategy is to ask good questions. How are you at asking questions that can shift a conversation?

Asking Powerful Questions

The quote on the right from Peter Block reminds us of the transformational possibilities of a good question. To begin this exploration of questions, here is a story of how my life was transformed with the power of a question:

> *Transformation comes more from pursuing profound questions than seeking practical answers.*
> – Peter Block

From Depression to Transformation with a Question

I returned from a wonderful sailing trip in the Caribbean with a group of friends, feeling depressed (this could not have been anticipated). The other three guys on the boat I was on all seemed so talented, and I was wondering what gifts I had to offer the world.

The people I spoke to all tried to comfort and reassure me, but I could not shake the feeling that I wasn't good enough.

Then, one of my colleagues said to me: "Yes, it would be wonderful to be as wise as Horst, as athletic and good-looking as Don, and as funny as Mike (the names have not been changed in order to honor the gifted), but would you trade your life with any of them?"

I thought about it for a minute and had one of those "aha" moments. The answer was no, as overall I liked myself and how my life was unfolding. This insight had a permanent impact, as I gained a heightened sense of myself in the process of answering the question.

The above story illustrates the power of a good question, and what it can mean for a friend, a family member, or in a session.

Many transformational questions are created in the moment, as in the above story. We can build our capacity to ask good questions by being curious and make inquisitiveness a way of being. Another way to build our capacity is to study transformational questions, and use them on ourselves and others.

Here are a few ideas for questions, followed by a section from some masters of asking good questions.

A Few Good Questions

Stimulating questions are a wonderful way of launching the journey of transformation. Here are a few examples:

- What is the one thing that you need to accomplish to make this year a success?
- What would one of your mentors or heroes do in this situation?
- Who needs to be in the session in order for you to be able to meet your objectives?
- Share an example of when you did something similar and were successful.
- What obstacles might you face, and how can you prepare yourself to overcome them?
- If you were successful, what would you be seeing, hearing, and feeling?
- What have you thought about doing and haven't done yet?
- On a scale of 1–10, how passionate are you about this idea?

You can tell whether a person is clever by their answers. You can tell whether a person is wise by their questions.
– Naguib Mahfouz

Who Are Some of the Experts on Questions?

A few authors have written masterfully on the subject of "Questions". Here are a few of them, along with some of their transformational questions:

Peter Block's *The Answer to How is Yes*

In his book, *The Answer to How is Yes,* he shows how we can shift our questions from a traditional style to ones with transformational attributes.

For example, "How long will it take?" can become "What commitment am I willing to make?", and "How have other people done it successfully?" can shift to "What do we want to create together?"

Last year I saw Peter facilitate a session at a conference. After the completion of small group discussions, he asked the large group, "What struck you in your conversations?"–"struck" is a word normally associated with lightning, which is a symbol of transformation. He shared that he invited transformation into the room when he asked that question.

Margaret Wheatley's *Turning to One Another*

"What do I believe about others?" and "What am I willing to notice in my world?" are among the questions to restore hope for the future.

John Scherer's *Five Questions that Change Everything: Life Lessons at Work*

In his aptly named book, John encourages us to look inside ourselves and ask: "What CONFRONTS me?", "What am I BRINGING?", "What RUNS me?", "What CALLS me?", and "What will UNLEASH me?"

Dick Whitney and Melissa Giovagnoli's *75 Cage-Rattling Questions to Change the Way You Work*

"What would your company be like if you never worked there?", "What unwritten rules make it difficult to get things done quickly, efficiently, or profitably?" and

"What question might you create to rattle the cages of the people you work with?" are some of the cage rattlers.

Dorothy Strachan's *Making Questions Work*

"What is one question you want answered by the end of this session?" and "How do other cultures approach this issue?" are just two of the stimulating questions from this master in the art of questions.

Leaders of the past were good at telling. Leaders of the future will be good at asking.
– Peter Drucker

These sample questions present a range of questions to enable us to spark stimulation in individuals and groups. These types of questions form a foundation that can support us in creating magical questions in the situations we encounter.

Summary

We have explored the three conditions of Dr Roger's "person-centered therapy": to be genuine, to give unconditional positive regard, and to display empathic understanding to others. We also added the dimension of asking powerful questions.

While we may not reach perfection in any of these four areas, we can continue to build our capacity for these qualities. This is a gift we can give to every person in our lives, from family members to people we meet on the street, and to participants we meet in sessions.

According to Dr Rogers, we play a pivotal role in the change process. As George Bernard Shaw said, "Keep yourself clean and bright. You are the window through which you must see the world."

Good leadership consists of doing less and being more.
– Lao Tze

Reflection Questions

Genuineness

1. How willing are you to be genuine, and to share your personal journey of applying the tools and concepts you facilitate?
2. Are you willing to be care-frontational with the groups you partner with?

Unconditional Positive Regard

3. What are you doing to increase your capacity to accept and love everyone you meet?
4. Are you able to see the "difficult" people in your life as your teachers?

Empathic Understanding

5. How are you at empathizing with people?
6. How are you at responding to participants who express emotions and opinions?

Ask Powerful Questions

7. How are you at asking questions that others find stimulating and transformational?
8. What are some of the specific questions you have found to be most useful in facilitating breakthrough insights?

Insights and Expansions

What did you find most interesting about this strategy?

How can you build your capacity to Be A Transformer?

___

___

Where to go from here?

If you would like to stay on the track of personal transformation, you might want to proceed to Strategy 11 "Seek and Celebrate Feedback". Otherwise, you could always place the table of contents on a table and drop something (nothing too messy) on it , to see where the object lands. Perhaps the object has some wisdom on which strategy is best for you to read next.

Strategy 10

BE GLOBAL AND LOCAL

We may have different religions, different languages,
different colored skin,
but we all belong to one human race.
– Kofi Annan

same same, but different.
– a popular saying and t-shirt slogan in Thailand

The strategies in this book seem to translate well; being intentional, being present, going for 100% and all the others, are strategies that have served me well in facilitating in more than 20 countries with participants from all around the world.

Differences in culture are considerations as we aspire to create transformation. Sometimes we might be working in a culture different from our own (country, region, or functional), and with content or a process that does not seem to naturally fit with the participant's culture. So in this strategy we will explore the challenge of being Global AND Local.

Here's the map for the strategy: we will begin our journey with some cross-cultural mistakes to learn from. After a stop for fuel, we will continue with our travel plan by exploring what being overly global or overly local might be like.

We will then follow the path to see what a blend of global and local might sound like, and how to walk the fine line between the two. We will complete our round-the-world trip with a few tips on working with cultures other than our own.

Cross-Cultural Mistakes and Lessons

Being culturally sensitive is part of the "Local" element in the title of this strategy. Most people who have traveled or worked in different countries have their favorite stories of cultural gaffes they have made. Do you have a favorite story that you have experienced or heard about when it comes to cross-cultural insensitivity? Well, these experiences in some ways teach us to be more sensitive in the future.

One of my gaffes happened during my first trip to Thailand. I was in an informal meeting with a number of Thai colleagues from AT&T, when I put my foot up on the table to tie my shoelace. I immediately knew by the look of shock on their faces that something was terribly wrong, but I didn't know what it was. Later, I was told that showing the bottom of your feet to people from Thailand is considered to be extremely rude.

It was only then that I remembered reading about this cultural tip in a guidebook, but it had slipped my mind. From that experience, I learned to read more about local customs, and to remember to follow them.

Cultural Diversity: More Than a Country

Cultural diversity not only spans across countries, but even within countries or across organizations and functions.

For me, growing up in New York/New Jersey in the U.S. and facilitating a session in Texas or Boston, is in some ways just as different as facilitating a session in Pakistan or Germany (perhaps even more so ☺).

Apart from the differences that arise from a change in geographical location, it is also useful to remember that each company and function has its own culture. Much of the advice that apply to countries also apply to individual companies and functions. For example, working with a group of engineers may seem like a different dimension of the universe, in comparison to working with a group of sales people (not that either group is deemed to be better or worse, if you are wondering). Even within a small country like Singapore, with a population of about 5 million people, there are significant differences between the cultures of local companies, governmental organizations, and multinational corporations.

As an example of company cultures, a friend told me that his Asia Leadership Team once fired a competent consultant in the middle of a session. Apparently, the consultant was trying to teach empowerment to a group of leaders in a company whose culture had already gone beyond empowerment. This is an extreme case of how understanding the culture of a company or function can be just as important as understanding country cultures.

The previous section points out that we have a variety of cross-cultural perspectives to select from in attempting to be Global and Local. On the next stop of our journey, we will zoom in on a particular context, where a facilitator from another part of the world comes to East Asia to facilitate a workshop.

Facilitating in East Asia: A Cross-Cultural Perspective

When visiting East Asia, some facilitators appear to be overly sensitive to local culture, while others do little to adjust their style and content. Mastery in this area is balancing and blending the best of all cultures, which is the exploration of this section. Let's see what these imbalances might look like, and get some ideas for blending the best of both worlds, literally and figuratively.

Too Much Local, Not Enough Global

Some facilitators are told that East Asian audiences prefer to listen, that they prefer not to participate. To be considerate of this preference, some speakers just download information to participants. While the intentions are good, such behavior reinforces the stereotype and does not offer participants an opportunity to speak up, share ideas, and become more engaged in the learning process.

However, in my experience, groups in East Asia require the structure and opportunity to participate. If you ask a group of 80 participants in Singapore or Thailand to share their thoughts in front of the entire group, you are likely to experience silence. However, if you provide smaller groups with a stimulating assignment, you will most likely see an amazing outpour of energy and creative ideas. Once a group warms up, participation opens up, even in the large group.

Too Much Global, Not Enough Local

Some facilitators conduct sessions in the same manner that they would in their home country. One such example is to preach total openness, which does not always translate well in East Asian culture.

Here is a quick example: A facilitator from outside Asia was in Singapore to conduct a session. During the session, some participants raised the question of how to go about facilitating if their CEO was one of the participants; they felt it was challenging to do this as internal staff who were much lower in the hierarchy of the organization. The facilitator insisted that CEOs should be treated the same as any other participant, and that it doesn't make any difference whether we are an internal or external facilitator.

His opinion was firm, and there was no discussion on how to deal with this situation. This is not meant to say that his opinion was right or wrong. It just seemed like a missed opportunity to engage in a dialogue on this important aspect of facilitation.

How to be Global AND Local?

So how do we avoid these traps of being overly global or local?

Here is one way to walk the fine line on this issue: "It is great to be here with you. I bring with me a wide range of tools and techniques that we will be exploring together and that will hopefully help you to be more effective. But what I don't have is a deep understanding of your culture. Thus, I would like your help to see how we can tailor these concepts, so they can fit into your cultural context."

This is a way to increase transformational learning and engage in a meaningful dialogue on the content. I have used variations of the above statement and have found that it does clarify the focus of the session. Of course, this approach runs the risk of getting off-track on questions about cultural relevance, but this is pertinent dialogue. And if everyone in the session agrees that some of the tools would not apply in their culture, then it is time to re-evaluate the tool or process, to explore modifications, or even to co-create a new model.

The following are two short instances of how a discussion on cross-cultural issues can be powerful and transformational. These are examples of how being Global AND Local can lead to breakthrough insights.

Two Examples of Cultural Relevancy Discussions

Is this Western Communication?

I was facilitating a session for facilitators in Singapore, practicing empathic listening skills (covered in Strategy 9 "Be a Transformer"). In the midst of the session, one of the participants stood up and shouted: "This is western communication, it's too soft. In Asia, we are very practical. We get to the point and don't waste time."

Being the only non-Asian in the room, I was not going to disagree with him. So I turned to the group for their opinion. The group members responded by clearly telling him that good listening skills are important in any culture. Upon hearing the feedback from his peers, he acknowledged the point, apologized to the group, and joined in the exercises.

Does 360 Degree Feedback Work in Asia?

During a leadership seminar which I attended, someone strongly protested to the use of 360 degree feedback in Asia. This participant claimed that the approach is inappropriate in the Asian context, as too much openness is simply not part of Asian culture.

Instead of disagreeing with the person and advocating for the use of such feedback, the facilitator asked everyone to share opinions and experiences.

What followed was a very rich dialogue on how and when to use the approach of 360 degree feedback in Asian organizations. Everyone gained a lot of insights from that exchange.

In the examples above, the groups were given the opportunity to dialogue on the issues in a meaningful way, and the interaction proved to be enriching and even transformational for some people. Sometimes the blend of Global AND Local is not quite as easy as opening up a discussion in the classroom. On occasion, the issue requires a lot more thoughtfulness and dialogue. Here is a story that illustrates how we can obtain a fine balance on cultural sensitivity, with a level of trust in some global principles, all in the spirit of creating purposeful transformation.

Cross-Cultural Transformation

I was co-facilitating a series of 4-day sessions for an organization in Thailand. One of the modules was designed for the participants to step out of their "Comfort Zone of Communication". They were given the opportunity to share appreciation, bring up problems, and make requests of one another.

When the Human Resource (HR) team in Thailand heard about this segment of the workshop, they told us that the concept was too western, and requested to replace that activity with something more culturally acceptable.

However, we had experienced transformational sessions with this "Comfort Zone of Communication" module in all the other countries we had worked in. We thought it could be more even powerful in a more conservative culture, as the process was very gentle and inviting. So, we met with the HR team and discussed how we could keep the module in the session, while at the same time honor Thai culture.

We agreed to place that module after dinner on the second day (it was a residential program). Groups sat in their functional teams and were invited to share things that were outside their "Comfort Zone of Communication". The participants were then given an option to stay for as short or long a time as they would like, and could do whatever they had wanted for the rest of the evening.

As we were staying in a beautiful resort, there were plenty of activities for them to do. In the first session with the Senior Leadership Team, they talked late into the night.

However, the senior leaders protested when we told them we were going to conduct this particular module organization-wide.

As much as they had enjoyed the open dialogue sessions, the senior leaders said the middle management and supervisory levels would not be able to deal with this type of openness in the Thai culture.

After further discussion on the overall purpose of the sessions and with a focus on the hopes for the corporate culture they aspired to create, it was decided that the module would be offered in the subsequent sessions. We continued to make it clear to the participants that they could leave the room anytime they wanted. We did this in all 10 sessions and almost without exception, the dialogues turned out to be long and meaningful. For many of the participants and teams, the module was the highlight of the four days.

Through this simple yet powerful exercise, the culture of this organization was transformed from a predominantly conservative Thai culture, to one where the leaders and staff made a conscious choice about the appropriate level of openness. They managed to integrate some western openness into Thai graciousness and politeness, as part of their corporate culture.

What is the moral of the story? Well, with enough dialogue and with a focus on the higher mission of the organization, it is possible to get the best of both worlds.

Challenges and Joys of Working with Diverse Groups

Sometimes it is a challenge to facilitate with a diverse groups of participants, especially when language is a barrier. To overcome a language challenge, one tip is to be sure that the ideas and instructions are on slides and charts as much as possible. It is often difficult for people to speak up if they did not understand the verbal instructions, so reading makes it so much easier for them.

We could learn a lot from crayons; some are sharp, some are pretty, some are dull, while others bright; some have weird names, but they have all learned to live together in the same box.
– Robert Fulghum

However, working with a diverse group presents wonderful learning opportunities, and can be lots of fun. I was once facilitating an Asia-wide conference and had lunch with a group of leaders from the Middle East, namely, Saudi Arabia, Kuwait, Egypt, and Iraq. As I was about to sit down at the table, one of them asked if I was ok to sit at the "terrorist table". I joined them, and they shared humorous stories of their experiences, being from the Middle East and working for a large global company.

Some Reminders for Working in Another Culture

Here is some simple advice: When you are about to facilitate a session in another culture, try to learn as much as you can about their styles, tendencies, learning preferences, as well as the general Do's and Don'ts. If you are facilitating in a country that speaks a different language, it helps to pick up some key phrases that you think might be relevant for your topic. It is also a good idea to read the local newspapers and the company website, to be in tune with the latest news.

In addition, music provides a good channel to connect with different cultures. A good friend, when facilitating in a country outside of his own, goes to a local CD shop upon arrival and asks for the most popular local music. The following day, he plays the music in the session, much to the pleasant surprise of the local folks.

Another cross-cultural tip has to do with talking politics and country culture. My experience is that most people around the world complain about their own governments and what is happening within their home country. However, these same people tend to react defensively when an external party criticizes their country. Thus, this is an area to proceed with caution.

Once you have learned as much cultural differences as you can, do what you do best when you are with the group, and remember the first four strategies of this book: "Be Intentional", "Be Present", "Go for 100%", and "Tune In And Engage".

Global Souls

Another interesting development in the area of cross-cultural issues is the growing number of people who have traveled and lived all around the world, which makes it counter-productive to label someone based on their ethnicity, or country of origin. For example, how do we classify an individual who has the following life resume: Indian ethnicity, early years in London, then lived on a farm in India, obtained degrees in the UK and US, and had long-term work assignments in China, Singapore, Germany and Indonesia?

In Pico Iyer's book entitled *The Global Soul*, the author describes more of such people in this wonderfully small and big world.

Summary

Our journey has taken us on a long trip, and fortunately, we were able to travel without being cramped in economy class on a long-haul flight. We first viewed some cross-cultural mistakes, followed by the reminder that cross-cultural considerations are relevant for both companies and functions. We also saw the consequences of facilitating in a manner that is overly global, or overly local. We then explored some examples of how to blend and integrate various cultural considerations, by opening dialogue for cultural relevancy of models and tools.

We completed our trip with some tips on how to increase the chances of enjoying an effective cross-cultural facilitation experience. Cheers to the wonderful diversity and opportunities of the global village we now inhabit. It has become clear that we are all neighbors and the more we understand each other and partner together, the better off we will all be.

Our lives are all different and yet the same.
– Anne Frank

Reflection Questions

1. What do you do to prepare yourself for working with or in another culture? (E.g., a new country, function, organization)?
2. How flexible are you in engaging participants in a way that balances and blends the global perspective with a local flavor?

Insights and Expansions

What did you find most interesting about this strategy?

____

____

How can you build your capacity to Be Global and Local?

____

____

Where to go from here?

If you have been reading the strategies in sequence, you have two more to explore. Otherwise, it might be time for you to pick your favorite technique of selecting a strategy, or make up a new one. Regardless of your technique, I hope that you are picking up useful reminders, and asking yourself some challenging questions.

Strategy 11

SEEK AND CELEBRATE FEEDBACK

The superior person encourages people to approach them by their readiness to receive them.
– I Ching

People say I don't take criticism very well, but I say "What the heck do they know?"
– Groucho Marx

If I am a good facilitator and lecturer, it is the result of the feedback I have received from colleagues and participants over the years (thanks everyone!). However, the ability to accept constructive feedback did not come naturally to me.

The willingness and ability to elegantly accept constructive feedback is an essential quality for improving ourselves as facilitators and human beings. We will explore ways to receive and celebrate feedback from others, as well as see the transformative impact of high levels of openness.

Giving and Receiving Feedback

I come from a family that is conservative in terms of communicating feedback. My academic background was in accounting and finance, followed by nine years working with computers and computer programmers in AT&T. In my family, as well as in professional domains, the focus of most conversations was not on the interpersonal side of things. Rather, the focus was on who won the game, how to get the numbers to balance, and how to get the programs to our customers on time.

We tend to judge others by their behaviors and ourselves by our intentions, and vice-versa.
– unknown

So when I first started in the facilitation profession, I was shocked by the many hours spent exchanging feedback every day. No kidding, every day we spent hours giving each other feedback.

We spent these hours sharing our observations of what went well or didn't go well. We discussed big issues, such as "I experienced your flow as disjointed", as well as the seemingly small ones, such as "you used the word 'game' instead of activity". We had a mission of co-creating miracles all over the world, so the continuous and rigorous flow of feedback served us well.

As stimulating and helpful as it was, this flow of constructive feedback at times created mixed emotions. I was happy to be getting feedback, but often felt defensive. Although positive feedback comprised about 50% of the comments, the areas for improvement seemed to carry more weight, and often created a sense of feeling hurt. Can you relate to this at all?

How Do You Respond to Feedback?

As a team, we became fascinated with this phenomena of giving and receiving feedback. Sometimes we took a break from sharing constructive feedback, and had positive-feedback-only debriefs. But we also knew that a lot of improvements came with the constructive feedback, and were intrigued by how we each responded to ideas for improvement. Intellectually, we knew that the feedback was useful; therefore, we knew we needed to work on the emotional aspect of hearing ideas for improvement.

If you are 100% fine with constructive feedback and do not feel the least sense of hurt when you receive such feedback, then congratulations. You may even want to skip this section.

Criticism can be hard to take, especially from a friend, a colleague, a family member, or a stranger.
– Franklin Jones

If you are still reading, imagine the following scenario: You have just facilitated a session and you are alone, reading the evaluation forms, when you come across a comment from a participant that reads: "The facilitator was not able to communicate the concepts clearly. I am still confused about the topic."

What is your internal self-talk after reading such a comment? Read the responses in Figure 11-1 and see if any of them sound familiar to you:

TYPE	RESPONSE
The DEFENDER /BLAMER	Yes, I am not surprised that this person is confused. I think that this person must be always confused, because I was crystal clear.
The RATIONALIZER	Well, these concepts are complex and will not be clear to everyone when they first hear it.
The SELF-PITY PERSON	Oh my, I am such a terrible communicator, and it's no wonder that some people don't get it. I should change profession.
The INTIMIDATOR	How dare this person write this about me. Let's do a handwriting analysis to find out who wrote this and I'll call them up to tell them to pay more attention next time, or to ask questions if they are not clear.

Figure 11-1: Types of internal self-talk *(continued)*

The SELF-ACTUALIZED PERSON	Isn't it interesting to get this feedback? I thought I was clear, but obviously I wasn't. If one person wrote this, there are probably others who were not clear but didn't take the time to write it. Let me think about how I can improve on this, so I can reach 100% the next time.

Figure 11-1: Types of internal self-talk *(continued)*

Is the self-actualized internal response realistic? Well, why not embrace it as an aspiration? Is it normal for some of the other reactions to come to mind from time to time when receiving constructive feedback? Probably. But how wonderful it is when participants take the time to share their thoughts and offer us some free advice to help us improve.

Celebrating Feedback

The previous scenario highlights a situation when we receive feedback through an evaluation form. But sometimes we receive verbal feedback from a participant or colleague. Imagine the courage and trust required for a person to give us critical feedback face-to-face. If someone is able to stand in front of us and tell us about what they do not like about our work, this demonstrates they trust us to accept the feedback in a positive manner. What a compliment! (Yes, it is paradoxical that constructive feedback is a compliment). Therefore, the next time someone gives you advice, remember to thank them for the trust, and to give yourself an internal pat on the back for being so trustworthy.

The following story illustrates the benefits of being open to feedback, and illustrates how this simple practice helps us to gain respect from the people we interact with.

Receiving Negative Feedback: What a Difference a Day Makes

Years ago, I was lecturing in Organization Theory at the Singapore Institute of Management (SIM). It was my first time lecturing in that subject, and the mid-semester evaluations from the students were quite average; the ratings were lower than normal, and the written comments indicated the students wanted more structure in the lectures (fair enough, considering that the subject was about organization structure), more substantive notes, as well as more examples that were relevant in Singapore.

In the following lesson, I provided the students with a summary of the feedback, thanked them for their openness, and shared with them how I would attempt to improve. By the end of the semester, the evaluations improved, although I still had adjustments to make for the following semester.

Because of my previous experiences with feedback, I thought nothing of what had happened; being open to feedback and then acting on it had become second nature to me.

It turned out that the following evening after I had been so open with them, one of the other lecturers berated the students for the bad feedback they had given him (this group must have had a tough semester). That lecturer had told the class that they were ungrateful for his efforts, and as a result, he was not going to help them anymore. Instead, he would just show up for class, lecture, and go home.

To this day, I do not know who that other lecturer was, but he made me look good. I guess I should appreciate this, but I would be happier if each of us could be more open to feedback.

Seeking Feedback

It is a rare person who wants to hear what they don't want to hear.
– Dick Cavett

By being open to feedback, we receive so much credit from participants, even more so when we make adjustments based on that feedback. So let's make it a point to reach out and get as much feedback as possible.

For example, when we facilitate a multiple day session, we can conclude each day by asking participants what they would like more or less of for the subsequent days. Such requests might include "more activities", "let's all be more open", or even "please provide better food for tea break".

Another methodology for receiving feedback in the middle of a session or semester is to conduct a quick survey. While some ideas might be BIG and others might be seemingly small, they are all important (part of Strategy 3 "Go for 100%").

Here is a story of one such survey and the subsequent adjustments made from the feedback:

Small Feedback Can Make a BIG Difference

I conducted a short survey to gather some feedback during the middle of a semester. One student wrote that she was sometimes distracted by some jiggling of coins in my pocket. Even though this was a simple piece of feedback, it was nevertheless impactful. Ever since that feedback, I have made it a point to empty my pockets of anything that might create noise during a session.

This little piece of feedback proved to be a BIG deal, as this person was able to focus her attention on learning, instead of being distracted by the noise made by some loose change. My guess is that many people over the years have benefitted from this, as the noise from my pockets have not been distracting participants.

Below is one more story which illustrates the positive consequences of being open to feedback.

Transforming with Feedback

It was the final night of a 1-year diploma program; all the lecturers and students from the program were gathered to celebrate the past year.

One of the lecturers had taught a subject in which he knew the theory, but did not have much practical experience. I had heard that he had some difficulties with the students, who were initially disappointed in his inability to deepen their understanding of the subject with tangible examples.

Toward the end of the gathering, each student had a chance to share their reflections of the past year. A few students thanked this particular lecturer for being so open to their feedback, and a few of them even cried as they expressed their appreciation for his effort. Apparently the lecturer responded favorably to the student's complaints, and managed to make some changes to help the students learn more on the topic.

By being so open and doing his best to accommodate the students, this lecturer transformed a potentially bad situation into a positive one. For all of us present, it was a memorable night. We experienced the appreciation and admiration the students had for this lecturer, after he had gotten off to a difficult start.

Just as the lecturer in the above story, how can we be more self-actualized in how we receive constructive feedback? Well, below are things you already know, so let's call them reminders about receiving feedback:

- Adopt the belief that ALL feedback is useful. Even if it seems irrelevant, or is attached with anger, each feedback presents its value for us to process and consider.
- See all feedback as data, information to think about, not necessarily positive or constructive.
- Do not get defensive. Ask questions and request for examples if you are unsure of what a participant is trying to communicate. Be sure to breathe, relax, and smile during the conversation.
- Make it easy for others to give feedback. Most people hesitate to share critical feedback, so be sure that our words and body language give a sense of safety and permission for others to be open and share their comments.

- Practice, practice, practice; sincerely ask for feedback, seek it out as much as possible, with open-ended questions.
- Ensure that course evaluations are designed for participants to provide improvement ideas for us and the course. This sounds like common sense, but it is sometimes not the case. Make use of this great tool for learning and expansion.
- In a session which spread over a few days, conduct a formal or informal feedback session at the end of each day.
- Pay attention to the verbal and non-verbal cues that others offer us in and out of the classroom. A tremendous amount of learning is available if we pay attention.
- Besides listening to feedback with an open mind, it helps if we make adjustments based on the feedback. Most feedback offer us the opportunity to do something different and show that we acted on the feedback.
- Remember that it is a compliment when someone trusts us enough to give us constructive feedback.

What About Positive Feedback?

At this juncture, some of you might be wondering why this strategy has focused solely on improvement feedback, without any mention of how to handle praise when it comes our way. We can also learn a lot from positive feedback, to be sure we are doing more of what supports participants and their learning.

So how do we handle positive feedback? Someone once said that our standard response to positive feedback ought to be "coming from you, that's quite a compliment", in order to return the favor. I don't think it makes sense to give a standard reply to compliments. After all, we have a variety of choices on how to deal with positive feedback, in ways that are meaningful and authentic. Sometimes compliments present us an opportunity to probe under the surface, to obtain more specific ideas about what supported the participant. This could be helpful both to them and ourselves. One other way of replying to a compliment is "thanks for that, please tell me more".

Summary

The main focus of this strategy is to enjoy getting our free, self-improvement tips, so that we can co-create even more transformation in the future.

Besides improving on ourselves through feedback, we can also be role models in this area. As I recollect my challenges in accepting feedback, I now hope that my openness will inspire others to be more receptive and less defensive when feedback comes their way (even though I am still working on this).

What feedback do you have for me? Please send your comments to dougo@jolc.com, thanks!

Everyone gets the experience. Some get the lesson.
– T.S. Eliot

Reflection Questions

1. How extensive and detailed is the feedback you receive through written evaluations?
2. Do you make it a habit to seek out people and ask questions like "How do you think I can be a better facilitator?" and/or "How can I make this course better?"
3. How are you at celebrating getting improvement tips from others?

Insights and Expansions

What did you find most interesting about this strategy?

____

____

How can you build your capacity to Seek and Celebrate Feedback?

Where to go from here?

If you are in the mood for something else, how about reading the strategy that matches the last digit of your telephone number.

The final strategy of the book is number 12, "Bring Your Whole Self to Work".

Strategy 12

BRING YOUR WHOLE SELF TO WORK

When it is all said and done, you are the instrument.
When the tools and techniques have run their course–
you were still the conduit.
When you engage with a system, half the coupling is you.
– Dave Jamieson

May the light at the core of your being illuminate the world.
– Kate Novak

This last strategy in the book serves as a reminder that who we are is a strategy for facilitating transformation. If the 12 strategies in this book represent a tapestry, then this strategy is the golden thread that weaves through the other 11.

In the following pages we will first explore facilitation as something we enjoy doing, rather than something that defines us. Next, we will move on to a poem and some questions, about who we are as facilitators and teachers, which are designed to spark some soul-searching reflections. We will complete the strategy with stories from some facilitators and teachers about how they bring who they are to what they do.

We Are More Than Our Work

There is a potential unintended consequence of being passionate about what we do. We could end up with a big part of our identity wrapped up in our role as facilitators and teachers.

I experienced a transformational insight about my identity, during a sabbatical I took several years ago. I didn't facilitate for six months, after almost 30 years of intense coaching, facilitating, and lecturing. I had gained so much satisfaction in my life through coaching and facilitating, that I had gradually come to fuse my work with my identity. So the "aha" was that I didn't have to be facilitating a workshop or lecture in order to feel totally alive and fulfilled.

Facilitating was something I enjoyed, but my life is more than playing the role of a facilitator. I returned from the sabbatical with a renewed sense of purpose and an expanded identity. I began to see myself as a joyous human being with many interests, and who happened to love coaching and facilitating.

I sometimes recognize others who seem to be wrapped up in their identity as a teacher or facilitator. I once co-facilitated a workshop with a school teacher, who was treating the adult participants as she would young children. When we debriefed the first day, she realized what she had been doing, and changed her style and approach on subsequent days.

When we limit our identity to our role as facilitator and teacher, we risk not meeting the group as fellow human beings on the journey of life. However, an expanded identity brings more empathy and presence to the groups we work with.

My hope for myself and for all of us who do this work, is that we remember to bring our whole self to work.

You Are the Instrument

So if facilitating is something we do rather than our identity, then who are we that engage with others? In the following sections, these questions will be asked in two different forms, by Dave Jamieson and Parker Palmer. This might be a good time to slow down and savor the next few pages.

One reflection for bringing ourselves to work comes from Dave Jamieson in his magnificent poem "You are the Instrument". Enjoy immersing yourself in this reminder of the role our "being" plays in our engagement with others.

YOU ARE THE INSTRUMENT

by Dave Jamieson

When it is all said and done, you are the instrument.
When the tools and techniques have run their course–you were still the conduit.
When you engage with a system, half the coupling is you.
When you respond to what's going on–your self is involved.
When others respond to what you are doing–it's never just what, but how.
While it's important to know theory and method, it's not enough–it's necessary but not sufficient.
What comes out, comes out through you...
  through your filters
  through your self-esteem
  through your fears
  through your skills
  through your needs
  through your personal turmoil
  through your presence.
Such an important and difficult accountability we take on...
  to be well-honed
  to be "in-shape" to practice the profession
  to be the best we can be
  to be a reflection of what's out there without distortion
  to be sensitive to adding value without having to be responsible for all
  to be tolerant of such great variability

You are the instrument of change, and that means knowing who you are...

how you touch people
your special qualities
what "hooks" you
how others gain from you
how you communicate with others
your way of giving
what you value and what you value blindly
what brings out the worst in you
when you're at your best
what you're working on personally
the selves inside of you
the spaces that you occupy
how you're influenced
when it's fun and when it's not
when you're "on" and when you're "off"
your need for structure and security
your repetitive patterns

Being an instrument of change is exciting, challenging, scary, fulfilling, engaging, intense, and rewarding.

Through our work we help others, and grow ourselves.

Because it's through self-insight, feedback, stretching encounters, and humility that we really learn how the instrument works and how it can be developed and used to make beautiful music!

Reproduced with permission from the author Dave Jamieson (thank you Professor!)

So who are you, the instrument that engages with others? Over and above the tools, processes, and knowledge you have acquired, who are you that shows up to partner with a group?

You may want to stop and reflect on this poem and these questions. When you are ready to move on, what follows is another way of asking these profound questions.

Who Are You That Teaches?

Parker Palmer is a mindful, passionate teacher who has supported teachers all around the world. In his insightful book *Courage to Teach,* he asks three questions of us:

1. What do you teach?
2. Why do you teach?
3. Who are you that teaches?

Let those questions percolate, as they are transformational in nature. The third question is one that we may never have an exact answer to, as it is the type of reflection we "grow into". "Who are you that teaches?" As Mahatma Gandhi said, "The teacher is the lesson." Parker Palmer's questions go right to the heart and soul of teaching. What are your heart and soul saying?

Hope you are enjoying the stimulation of the questions in this strategy. Next up are some stories which answer a similar question, "What is it you bring to your work, as a teacher and facilitator?" .

What Is It That You Bring to "Work"– Examples from Teachers and Facilitators

I asked a few teachers and facilitators whom I admire, to share with us how they bring their whole self to work. Over the next few pages, I hope you enjoy their thoughtful stories, and that you will be thinking about what you bring to your work with groups.

When we try to pick up anything by itself, we find it hitched to everything else in the universe.
– John Muir

What I Bring: PASSION AND HARD WORK

My life has taught me through personal experience, and from watching others, that the more you put into something, the more you get out of it. So putting my heart and soul into my teaching/coaching reaps both long-term and immediate results for student and teacher. The passion I share for a particular subject/training area is contagious because it comes from a place that is real! Currently my job allows me to learn every day from teenagers; I learn from watching, from listening or from just being with them! It is this learning that helps continue the process of growth for myself and the students, and reinforces that passion and hard work create meaningful rewards for everyone. I have been blessed in so many ways, thus creating opportunity to forever keep the passion in what I can bring to "work" every day!

– **Peggy Bionde**
Pequannock High School Teacher and Basketball Coach, New Jersey

What I Bring: LESSONS FROM HOME

I grew up in an era when my father was the "man of the house", and as children, our job was to listen and take orders. As a husband and father in current times, I obviously have seen that those expectations have changed. My wife and I are equal partners, and my two daughters want their opinions to count and their voices to be heard.

From my wife, I learned the value of feedback, as we can always improve ourselves further. The four of us give a lot of feedback to one another, and it has created a family culture of openness, trust and learning. I therefore make it a point to always ask my clients what they think of my work. If they tell me it's good, I know what I have done right. If they tell me otherwise, I know where I need to improve.

From my daughters, I have developed patience and empathy, and learned the skills of engagement, involvement and empowerment. When I facilitate a session, I go with the belief that the participants have their own answers and perspectives of the issue being discussed. With my daughters and with participants, my role is to help them connect the dots so that they can develop a sense of confidence and achievement in arriving at a decision. They are also more likely to commit to the solutions they create.

My family has taught me so much that has added tremendous value to the perspectives I take when I facilitate.

– **Ling Yuin Fong**
Open Dimensions, Singapore

What I Bring: MY LIFE MISSION

Throughout my life I have constantly asked myself, "When people think of Prabu Naidu, what would come to their minds?" This question has served me well, especially in the last 10 years as an independent consultant and facilitator. I want to be known as someone who will do whatever it takes to serve my clients, and want to be known as someone who has contributed to the community and made a difference.

These passions have helped me to strive to deliver beyond expectations. My clients trust me and know that I will do whatever it takes to serve them. It also drove me to co-found the Facilitators Network Singapore (FNS) with Janice Lua. We are striving to create a multiplier effect: building up the level of facilitation in Singapore and Asia, through collaborative and consultative approaches. I am sure that our efforts will further contribute to a better society in Asia, and hopefully I will be remembered as someone who went beyond expectations and contributed to society in some way.

– **Prabu Naidu**
Learning Matters, Co-founder of the Facilitators Network of Singapore (FNS)
Singapore

What We Bring: PASSION FOR LEARNING

Every year, we travel somewhere in the world for what we call the "first dip of the tea bag". This means we go directly to the source of a model or set of tools which we have heard about and find stimulating. We love to learn new things. What we then bring to the organizations and people we work with is an extensive menu of possibilities that can support them in their development. We also hope that our passion for learning new things is contagious.

– **Aart and Loes Pijl**
Change Company, Netherlands

What I Bring: COURAGE AND AUTHENTICITY

As a counselor, I had begun the practice of starting each individual or group session with the ringing of meditation bells, some deep breaths and a check-in about what was foreground in their awareness.

When I got my first project as an organization consultant, I decided to bring some of the practices that had helped my counseling clients. I took a deep breath and told the group that it was my practice to start meetings with a few minutes of silence. I ignored the frowns and darting eyes, and rang the bells. I could feel every one of my thunderous heartbeats in those two minutes. Was I crazy? What made me think that these folks could even sit still for two minutes? I resisted looking at my watch. I counted my breaths until I reached two minutes worth.

When I opened my eyes, I said that I would go first to model what I meant by "check-in". It was the moment of truth. Would I be honest about how I was feeling, or would I give them some platitudes that would make me look like I had it all together? I took another deep breath. "That was the hardest two minutes I can remember. I am so grateful that you are all still sitting here." The group laughed, and then each person in that circle then shared something that they had never told their co-workers before.

Those sacred bells are still with me, and have accompanied me in my travels as an organization consultant. They remind me to be courageous and authentic, and they can tell many stories of hope and transformation.

– **Christine Whitney-Sanchez**
Collaborative Wisdom and Strategy (CWS), Arizona

What I Bring: THE PARADOX OF SELF

The times when I have enjoyed facilitating the most and did some of my most transformational work was when I was able to forget the "self" in the "work". I find that I have to work hard to get my "self" out of the way, and focus single-mindedly on the purpose of the session or the intervention. The more I am able to do that, the more present I can be, to attend to what needs attention in the moment. As I go about serving whoever is in the room, that in turn helps them focus their own sense of purpose and mission. This is the paradox of self, that I get my "self" out of the way to maximize effectiveness and transformation.

– **Jacqueline Wong**
Sequoia Consulting, Singapore

As for me, what I bring is my desire to make my last shot. When I was growing up and playing a lot of basketball, we had a ritual of making our last shot before leaving the court. One day, the significance of the ritual occurred to me; if we were to die before we made it back to the courts, we would have at least passed over to the other side, knowing that we had made our "last shot".

I took this ritual and lesson along to my work as a facilitator. I commit myself to making my last shot in as many areas of life as possible, such as facilitating a session. Being in the role of teacher or facilitator is a sacred experience, and we never know which session will be our last. So I treat every session with a group as if it will be my last time with them (I don't tell them this, as I am still hopeful there will be more). Mahatma Gandhi summed up this "make the last shot" idea with his quote, "Live as if this will be your last day. Learn as if you are going to live forever."

My wish is that each of us can "make our last shot". I hope that in some way, these stories and this book has served you on your journey of making this happen.

Summary

This strategy is a reminder that *who* we bring to others is a strategy in and of itself. It started with a reminder not to get too attached to being a facilitator, but to be a human being who enjoys facilitating. "You Are the Instrument" and "Who Are You That Teaches?" stimulated some soulful reflections. We concluded with a few stories of how others bring their "self" to work.

Here is a test to find if your mission on earth is finished;
if you are alive, it isn't.
– Mother Theresa

Reflection Questions

1. Who are you, the instrument, that facilitates?
2. What would be your story of how you bring your whole self to your work?

Insights and Expansions

What did you find most interesting about this strategy?

____

____

How can you build your capacity to Bring Your Whole Self to Work?

____

____

Where to go from here?

If this is the first strategy that you are reading, I hope this has given you context for further exploration. If you are randomly reading strategies that capture your interest or attention, continue on this path and stay light for the journey ahead.

If you have finished reading the book, it is now time to place your insights into action, or re-read a strategy that does not feel complete for you. Throughout this journey, remember to celebrate your successes and focus on learning from setbacks (a lesson from Strategy 7 "Mind Your Language").

EPILOGUE

The 12 strategies presented in this book are not separate aspects of facilitation, but part of a larger tapestry that facilitates transformation. As we hone our attention and skills on any of the strategies, we expand our capacity to create breakthroughs with others.

The 12 strategies of the tapestry do not represent the complete range of possibilities for topics. For example, the use of technology for transformation would be a strategy worth exploring, or how topics such as adult developmental psychology and neuroscience can contribute to our understanding of learning and change. Also, helping to enhance the sustainability of sessions is a topic worthy of another book; in this book we covered it briefly in the context of the language strategy. What strategies would you add or modify?

If you are wondering whether we have to be proficient in all the 12 strategies in order to facilitate transformation, the good news is that the answer is no. Well, it would be great if we are masterful at all the strategies, but even in that case there would always be higher levels of mastery to attain.

The bonus is that as we expand our capacity in these strategies, we experience and facilitate even more transformation, for others and for ourselves. This is the upward spiral that is represented on the cover of the book. What are the one or two strategies which will supply you the most leverage on your upward spiral of facilitating transformation?

"Facilitating Transformation" is a topic that brings with it lots of questions and possibilities for enriching reflection and dialogue. If you have any questions, feedback, or ideas, please send an email to me at dougo@jolc.com.

I look forward to hearing from you.

ACKNOWLEDGEMENTS

To EACH and ALL of the participants, students, and co-facilitators with whom I have shared part of the learning journey, thanks for all the lessons and insights we have shared along the way. It has been a joy and a privilege.

To Horst Abraham, thanks for the guidance and strong foundation you provided for me and for our AT&T Project Miracles team. Thanks to each of the Project Miracles team members in the U.S., Singapore, and Thailand, for the passion and learning we brought to one another and to the world. Our work together lives on in many different forms.

To Marvin Weisbord and Sandra Janoff of the Future Search Network, thanks for showing the way for what masterful facilitation looks like, and for so generously and passionately sharing the principles on which your work is based. Thank you Sandra for writing such an elegant foreword, and for putting the book in such an expansive context.

To each of you who were willing to write a review for the book, or a story for Strategy 12, thank you!

To those of you who read drafts of the book and gave detailed feedback: Michael Boey, Doug Brockbank, Sandra Janoff, Anisha Kaul, Lisa Lee, Ling Yuin Fong, John Mauro, Jeff Ong, and Dustin Woods. If this book makes sense, it is because of you. I appreciate your energy, insights, and friendship.

To Prabu Naidu, you have been magically part of two significant events in my life; my "accidentally" ending up in Singapore, and having a practical reason to complete this book. Thanks a lot Naidu!

To Phoon Kok Hwa, thanks for your extraordinary partnership. As a publisher, your personalized and professional service exceeded my already high expectations. To Corrine Teng, thanks for providing me with hope; first by believing in the book, and then by giving the draft a structure and style worthy of publication.

To Dilip Mukerjea, you read the first draft of the book years ago, and saw good ideas wrapped in bad writing. Thanks Bro for the feedback! Hope this version is easier to read.

To Mom and Dad, thanks for always being so supportive and loving. You always told us to follow our hearts and to get a good education. Thanks for everything!

To Christy, I appreciate the many hours we have spent bouncing around ideas for this book. Thanks for teaching me so much about transformation along the way. I used to dream of a perfect partner, and you are better than my dream come true.

TRANSFORMATIONAL REFERENCES

Some of the items below were referenced in the text and others were included for their transformational capacity. The works of all authors mentioned in the text are referenced in their respective strategies, though a number of books could have been used in multiple sections.

The quotations in this book were collected from a wide variety of sources over the years... emails, books, websites, calendars, magazines, train stations, etc. I appreciate and honor each and all of the "quote masters"; to distil such wisdom in a quote is an act of concentrated transformation.

Introduction

http://dictionary.reference.com/browse/transform

Dalmar Fisher, David Rooke, and Bill Torbet, *Personal and Organizational Transformation using Action Inquiry*, Edge/Work Press, 2003.

Robert Fritz, *The Path of Least Resistance for Managers: Designing Organizations to Succeed*, Berrett-Koehler, 1999.

Malcolm Gladwell, *Tipping Point*, Abacus, 2000.

Clare Graves, Chris Cowan and Natasha Todorovic, *The Neverending Quest: Dr Clare Graves Explores Human Nature*, ECLET Publishing, 2005.

James Heskett, Earl Sasser, and Leonard Schlesinger, *The Service Profit Chain*, Free Press, 1997.

Robert Kegan and Lisa Lahey, *Immunity to Change: How to Overcome It and Unlock the Potential in Yourself and Your Organization (Leadership for the Common Good)*, Harvard Business School Press, 2009.

Robert Kegan, *In Over Our Heads: The Mental Demands of Modern Life*, Harvard University Press, 1998.

Trina Paulus, *Hope for the Flowers: A tale... partly about revolution and lots about hope for adults and others (including caterpillars who can read)*, Paulist Press, 1972.

Robert Quinn, *Deep Change: Discovering the Leader Within*, Jossey-Bass, 1996.

Bill Torbert, *Action Inquiry: The Secret of Timely and Transforming Leadership*, Berrett-Kohler, 2004.

Marvin Weisbord, *Productive Workplaces Revisited: Dignity, Meaning, and Community in the 21st Century*, Jossey-Bass, 2004.

Strategy 1. Be Intentional

Wayne Dyer, *The Power of Intention*, Hay House, 2005.

Gordon MacKenzie, *Orbiting the Giant Hairball: A Corporate Fool's Guide to Corporate Survival*, Viking, 1998.

Strategy 2. Be Present with Presence

Belle Linda Halpern and Kathy Lubar, *Leadership Presence: Dramatic Techniques to Reach Out, Motivate, and Inspire*, Gotham, 2004.

Spencer Johnson, *The Present*, Doubleday, 2003.

Roger Schwarz, *The Skilled Facilitator: A Comprehensive Resource for Consultants, Facilitators, Managers, Trainers, and Coaches*, Jossey-Bass, 2002.

Eckhart Tolle, *The Power of Now: A Guide to Spiritual Enlightenment*, New World Library, 2004.

Strategy 3. Go for 100%

Scott Adams, *It's not Funny if I Have to Explain it: A Dilbert Treasury*, Andrew McMeel Publishing, 2004. (Note: there are many other "Dilbert" books by Scott Adams)

Judy Ringer, *Unlikely Teachers: Finding the Hidden Gifts in Daily Conflict*, OnePoint Press, 2006.

Marvin Weisbord and Sandra Janoff, *Don't Just Do Something, Stand There: Ten Principles for Leading Meetings that Matter*, Berrett-Koehler, 2007.

Strategy 4. Tune In and Engage

Chris Cowan and Don Beck, *Spiral Dynamics: Mastering Values, Leadership, and Change*, Wiley-Blackwell, 2005.

Howard Gardner, *Multiple Intelligences: New Horizons in Theory and Practice*, Basic Books, 2006.

David Kolb, *Experiential Learning: Experience as the Source of Learning and Development*, Prentice-Hall, 1983.

Michael Marquardt, *Optimizing the Power of Action Learning: Solving Problems and Building Leaders in Real Time*, Davies-Black Publishing, 2004.

Joseph O'Connor, *NLP Workbook: A Practical Guide to Achieving the Results You Want*, Thorsons, 2001.

Strategy 5. Design for Transformation

Barbara Bunker and Billie Albans, *Large Group Interventions: Engaging the Whole System for Rapid Change*, Jossey-Bass, 1997.

Barbara Bunker and Billie Albans, *The Handbook of Large Group Methods: Creating Systemic Change in Organizations and Communities*, Jossey-Bass, 2006.

Center for Creative Leadership (CCL), http://www.ccl.org

David Cooperrider, Diana Whitley, and Jacqueline Stavros, *The Appreciative Inquiry Handbook: For Leaders of Change*, Berrett-Koehler, 2008.

Peggy Holman, Steve Cady, and Tom Devane, *Change Handbook: The Definitive Resource on Today's Best Methods for Engaging Large Systems*, Berrett-Koehler, 2006.

Harrison Owen, *Open Space Technology: A User's Guide*, Berrett-Koehler, 2008.

Jeffrey Pfeffer and Robert Sutton, *The Knowing-Doing Gap: How Smart Companies Turn Knowledge into Action*, Harvard Business School Press, 2000.

Jim Rough, Dynamic Facilitation, http://www.tobe.net

Ricardo Semler, *The Seven-Day Weekend: Changing the Way Work Works*, Portfolio, 2004.

Marvin Weisbord and Sandra Janoff, *Future Search: An Action Guide to Finding Common Ground in Organizations and Communities*, Berrett-Koehler, 2000.

Strategy 6. Design the Environment

Juanita Brown and David Isaacs, *The World Café: Shaping Our Futures Through Conversations That Matter*, Berrett-Koehler, 2005.

Despair, Inc., http://www.despair.com

International Forum of Visual Practitioners, http://www.ifvp.org

Nancy Marguiles and Christine Valenza, *Visual Thinking: Tools for Mapping Your Ideas,* Crown House Publishing, 2005.

Will Schutz, *The Human Element: Productivity, Self-Esteem, and the Bottom Line*, Jossey-Bass, 1994.

Milly Sonneman, *Beyond Words: A Guide to Drawing Out Ideas*, Ten Speed Press, 1997.

Strategy 7. Mind Your Language

Jean Houston, *A Mythic Life*, HarperCollins, 1996.

Martin Seligman, *Learned Optimism: How to Change Your Mind and Your Life*, Vintage, 2006.

Martin Seligman, *The Optimistic Child: A Proven Program to Safeguard Children Against Depression and Build Lifelong Resilience*, Mariner Books, 2007.

Strategy 8. Breakthrough with Teams

Richard Beckhard, *Optimizing Team Building Effort, Journal of Contemporary Business*, 1972, Vol. 1, Issue 3.

Peter Block, *Flawless Consulting: A Guide to Getting Your Expertise Used*, Jossey-Bass, 2000.

Peter Block and Andrea Markowitz, *The Flawless Consulting Fieldbook and Companion: A Guide to Understanding Your Expertise*, Pfeiffer, 2000.

Peter Block, *Community: The Structure of Belonging*, Berrett-Koehler, 2008.

Patrick Lencioni, *Five Dysfunctions of a Team: A Leadership Fable*, Jossey-Bass, 2002.

Patrick Lencioni, *Four Obsessions of an Extraordinary Executive: A Leadership Fable*, Jossey-Bass, 2000.

Peter Senge, Charlotte Roberts, Richard Ross, and Bryan Smith, *Fifth Discipline Fieldbook: Strategies and Tools for Building a Learning Organization*, Nicholas Brealey, 1994.

Bruce Tuckman and Mary Ann Jensen, "Stages of small group development revisited", *Group and Organizational Studies*, 2, 419-427.

Strategy 9. Be a Transformer

Peter Block, *The Answer to How is Yes: Acting on What Matters*, Berrett-Koehler, 2003.

Viktor Frankl, *Man's Search for Meaning*, Beacon Press, 2006.

Michael Marquardt, *Leading with Questions: How Leaders Find the Right Solutions by Knowing What to Ask*, Jossey-Bass, 2005.

Carl Rogers, *A Way of Being*, Mariner Books, 1980.

Carl Rogers, *On Becoming a Person: A Therapist's View to Psychotherapy*, Mariner Books, 1995.

John Scherer, *Five Questions that Change Everything: Life Lessons at Work*, Word Keepers, 2009.

Dorothy Strachan, *Making Questions Work: A Guide to What and How to ask for Facilitators, Consultants, Managers, Coaches, and Educators*, Jossey-Bass, 2007.

Margaret Wheatley, *Turning to One Another: Simple Conversations to Restore Hope to the Future*, Berrett-Koehler, 2002.

Dick Whitney and Melissa Giovagnoli, *75 Cage-Rattling Questions to Change the Way You Work*, McGraw-Hill, 1997.

Strategy 10. Be Global AND Local

Roger Axtell, Essential *Do's and Taboos: The Complete Guide to International Business and Leisure Travel,* Wiley, 2007.

Geert Hofstede, *Cultures and Organizations: Software of the Mind,* McGraw-Hill, 2004, and http://www.geert-hofstede.com

Pico Iyer, *The Global Soul: Jet Lag, Shopping Malls, and the Search for Home,* Vintage, 2001.

Strategy 11. Seek and Celebrate Feedback

Joseph Folkman, *The Power of Feedback: 35 Principles for Turning Feedback from Others into Personal and Professional Change,* Wiley, 2006.

Karen Kirkland and Sam Manoogian, *Ongoing Feedback: How to Get It, How to Use It,* Center for Creative Leadership, 1998.

Susan Weitzel, *Feedback that Works: How to Build and Deliver Your Message,* Center for Creative Leadership, 2000.

Strategy 12. Bring Your Whole Self to Work

Geoffrey Bellman, *The Consultant's Calling: Bringing Who You Are to What You Do, Jossey-Bass, 2001.*

Oriah Mountain Dreamer, *The Invitation,* Harper, 1999.

Elisabeth Kubler-Ross and David Kessler, *Life Lessons: Two Experts on Death and Dying Teach Us About the Mysteries of Life and Living,* Scribner, 2000.

Donald Van Eynde, Judith Hoy and Dixie Cody Van Eynde, *Organization Development Classics,* Jossey-Bass, 1997.

ABOUT THE AUTHOR

Douglas O'Loughlin runs Joy of Learning Consultants, which he started in Singapore in 1993. He fortuitously entered the world of facilitation more than 20 years ago while working at AT&T in the U.S., and has since facilitated workshops in more than 20 countries. His expertise is to consult, design and facilitate sessions in areas such as change, leadership/ team/organization development, expansive/dynamic thinking, strategic planning, and facilitation.

He is also an adjunct facilitator and coach with the Center for Creative Leadership (CCL), an Associate with Harthill Consulting, and is involved with learning communities all over the world. Douglas lectured at the Singapore Institute of Management for 10 years in various subjects that start with "O" (Organization Behavior, Development, Effectiveness, and Theory).

He is currently doing a PhD in Organization Development, researching how the field of adult developmental psychology can accelerate leadership development. Douglas also lectures in the Masters of Management and Organization Development, at Assumption University in Bangkok.

Originally from the New York/New Jersey area in the U.S., he currently resides in both Singapore and Bangkok. He is married to Christy and they are joyfully engaged in supporting each other and working together. They don't have any children or pets, but they share their life with a magical character named Drax the Dragon.

http://www.jolc.com

7772011R00109

Made in the USA
San Bernardino, CA
16 January 2014